PERGAMON INSTITUTE OF ENGLISH
(NEW YORK)

Materials for Language Practice

COMMUNICATING IN ENGLISH

EXAMPLES AND MODELS

3 Situations

DEPARTMENT OF APPLIED LANGUAGE STUDIES

COMMUNICATING IN ENGLISH: EXAMPLES AND MODELS *is a three-volume series for high intermediate and advanced students of English as a Second or Foreign Language. The three volumes, written by Walter Matreyek and published by Pergamon Press, are:*
- Book 1: Functions
- Book 2: Notions
- Book 3: Situations

Other textbooks already published in our Materials for Language Practice Series for the student of American English:

ENGLISH AS AN INTERNATIONAL LANGUAGE: Eva S. Weiner and Larry E. Smith
A workbook which focuses on writing activities, which are also used as a base for the practice of the other skills. Its strong international flavor promotes students' understanding of different cultures.
0 08 030322 6f

PINT'S PASSAGES FOR AURAL COMPREHENSION: John Pint
Two books providing an ingenious combination of aural comprehension and cloze exercises.

TWENTIETH CENTURY NEWS
0 08 028620 8f
0 08 029430 8a Cassette kit (*book and cassette*)

TELEPHONE TALK
0 08 028621 6f
0 08 029455 3a Cassette kit (*book and cassette*)

READING SKILLS FOR THE FUTURE: Susan Lebauer
A systematic text designed to improve the reading skills of the student or professional; centred around the theme of energy resources.
0 08 028619 4f

TALK AND LISTEN: Richard Via and Larry E. Smith
English as an international language via drama techniques. Emphasis is placed on developing grammatical acceptability and social appropriateness. Practice goes all the way from simple dialogues to detailed roleplays.
0 08 030323 4f *Students' Book*
0 08 029448 0f *Teachers' Book*

YOSHI GOES TO NEW YORK: John Battaglia and Marilyn Fisher
Unscripted conversations with a businessman in New York is the story line. Authentic conversations and authentic materials combine to provide a course with wide appeal to all students regardless of nationality.
0 08 028648 8f
0 08 028665 8a Cassette kit (*book and cassette*)

COMMUNICATING IN ENGLISH

EXAMPLES AND MODELS

3 Situations

International Edition

Walter Matreyek

PERGAMON PRESS
New York · Oxford · Toronto · Sydney · Frankfurt

U.S.A.	Pergamon Press Inc., Maxwell House, Fairview Park, Elmsford, New York 10523, U.S.A.
U.K.	Pergamon Press Ltd., Headington Hill Hall, Oxford OX3 0BW, England
CANADA	Pergamon Press Canada Ltd., Suite 104, 150 Consumers Road, Willowdale, Ontario M2J 1P9, Canada
AUSTRALIA	Pergamon Press (Aust.) Pty. Ltd., P.O. Box 544, Potts Point, N.S.W. 2011, Australia
FEDERAL REPUBLIC OF GERMANY	Pergamon Press GmbH, Hammerweg 6, D-6242 Kronberg, Federal Republic of Germany
JAPAN	Pergamon Press Ltd., 8th Floor, Matsuoka Central Building, 1-7-1 Nishishinjuku, Shinjuku-ku, Tokyo 160, Japan
BRAZIL	Pergamon Editora Ltda., Rua Eça de Queiros, 346, CEP 04011, São Paulo, Brazil
PEOPLE'S REPUBLIC OF CHINA	Pergamon Press, Qianmen Hotel, Beijing, People's Republic of China

Copyright © 1983 Pergamon Press Inc.
Illustrations © 1983 Ian Kellas

All Rights Reserved. No part of this publication may be reproduced, stored in a retrieval system or transmitted in any form or by any means: electronic, electrostatic, magnetic tape, mechanical, photocopying, recording or otherwise, without permission in writing from the publishers.

First edition 1983
Reprinted (with corrections) 1986

Library of Congress Cataloging in Publication Data
Matreyek, Walter.
Communicating in English.
(Materials for language practice)
"A Flamm/Northam book" — T.p. verso.
Includes index.
Contents: 1. Interpersonal functions — 2. Semantic functions — 3. Conversation techniques, topics and situations.
1. English language — Text-books for foreigners.
2. English language — Spoken English. I. Title II. Series.
PE1128.M354   1983   428.2'4   82-15006

British Library Cataloguing in Publication Data
Matreyek, Walter
Communicating in English: examples and models.
(Materials for language practice)
Vol. 3 Situations
1. English language — Text-books for foreigners
I. Title   II. Series
428.2'4   PE1128
ISBN 0 08 028618 6

Printed in Great Britain by A. Wheaton & Co. Ltd., Exeter

Contents

Students' Introduction — vii
Teachers' Introduction — viii

CHAPTER 1: CONVERSATION TECHNIQUES — 1

1 Opening and Closing a Conversation — 2
2 Asking about/Expressing Opinions — 8
3 Regulating Other People's Speech:
  Repetition/Speed/Volume — 12
4 Asking for/Providing Meaning and Clarification — 15
5 Reflection — 18
6 Commentary — 21
7 Interrupting — 23
8 Checking Understanding/Clearing up Misunderstanding — 25
9 The Topic of Conversation: Changing/Returning to/
  Preventing a Change/Avoiding — 27
10 Bringing up an Idea/Adding Related Points — 31

CHAPTER 2: CONVERSATION TOPICS — 33

1 Weather — 33
2 Sightseeing — 36
3 Common Friends — 38
4 Origins/Home/Family — 40
5 Jobs and Work — 42
6 Free-Time Hobbies/Interests — 44
7 Past Experiences/Future Plans — 46
8 Vacations/Travel — 48
9 Education — 50
10 Everyday Problems — 52
11 Health and Illness — 54
12 Pets — 56
13 Food — 58
14 Clothes and Accessories — 60
15 Homes: Furniture and Decor — 62

CONTENTS

CHAPTER 3: SITUATIONS 64

A. Relations with Other People 64
    1 Greetings and Farewells 65
    2 Introductions 67
    3 Invitations 70
    4 Entertaining Visitors/Visiting People 72
    5 Dinner at Someone's Home 75

B. Necessities of Life 78
    1 Information 78
    2 Directions 80
    3 Business Appointments/Reception Desk 82
    4 Shopping 85
    5 Restaurants 88
    6 Doctor/Dentist/Hospital/Pharmacy 92
    7 Services: Barber/Beauty Shop/Cleaners 96
    8 Cars: Gas/Service 99
    9 Beggars/Salespeople/Solicitors/Proselytizers 101
    10 Bargaining: Flea Market/Garage Sales/ Second-Hand Shops 103

C. Public Services 105
    1 Telephone/Telegram 105
    2 Emergencies: Medical/Fire/Police 108
    3 Public Transportation: Bus and Taxi 110
    4 Bank 113
    5 Post Office 116

D. Travel 118
    1 Travel Agency 118
    2 Check-In/Ticket Counter 121
    3 Hotels/Motels 123
    4 Rental Cars 126

APPENDIX 1: PRELIMINARY ACTIVITIES 129
APPENDIX 2: SUGGESTED TECHNIQUES 133

Students' Introduction

We learn a new language in order to use it. We use it to have conversations and discussions with other people. We also use it to take care of the many everyday life situations we face.

This book can help you to take part in conversations and discussions and to take care of many everyday life situations more easily. You will work on some conversation techniques which you can use to begin, continue, change, and end conversations. You will also see how people talk about some common topics of convesation. In addition, you will work on words and expressions used in a number of everyday life situations, and also see what some people really say in these situations.

Whether you use this book for self-study or as a text in an English class, the responsibility for learning and using the words and expressions which you study is yours. You will need to read, to try to understand, and to try to use the words and expressions in the examples and models. In class, the teacher can help you by creating opportunities to use and learn them. But only you can decide to *really* learn and use them. You will probably make mistakes. But you will learn from your mistakes. Try to profit from the correction you receive from the teacher and others in order to improve your English.

I hope that you enjoy the book. I have tried to make it an interesting book for you. I have tried to make it a book from which you can learn a lot. I hope that you do. Good luck.

Walter Matreyek

Seattle, Washington, USA

Teachers' Introduction

This is a text in conversational and situational English for intermediate and advanced students. It focuses on the language that people use in everyday-life communications. It is designed for people who have some background in English, but who also have gaps, lack of variety or other problems in using English to communicate in everyday life.

This text is written to develop active, aware and independent learners. It is a performance-oriented text, so students need to read, think about, discuss and practice and perform the Examples, Models and Suggested Activities in each lesson. In doing so, they actively internalize the language related to the conversation techniques, conversations and situations in the book so that they can use them in everyday life. The Preliminary Activities in Appendix 1 and the Suggested Techniques in Appendix 2 will help develop and promote this active learning.

In addition, the text helps to develop aware learners: people who can recognize a particular situation and what is being called for as a response to the situation. Students begin to think about how to make an appropriate desired initiative or response, rather than how to come up with a grammatically correct sentence or question. Lastly, the present text is one that students can learn to use by themselves, independently, outside of class or after class has finished. If we can help students to become active, aware and independent learners, we are helping them to become people who can use English to accomplish what they want to in English.

Format of Lessons

The text is divided into three chapters with varying numbers of lessons. Each lesson is divided into three sections: Examples, Models and Suggested Activities. *Examples* are expressions, sentences or questions which show how the particular function in each lesson is used in everyday life. Models are conversation and discussion excerpts which place some of the examples in larger everyday contexts. Suggested Activities are problem-solving situations where the students have to apply what they've just learned in the Examples and Models sections in less-structured ways.

There are three things to keep in mind when using the text:
(1) Not all possible examples of the conversation techniques and situation turning-points are given in each lesson. Rather, the examples are limited to the most common and direct ones. This is because the text would soon become too long and unmanageable if all the subtle and indirect ways to express the function were given.

(2) Students will need to understand when and how to use various examples. They need to understand which forms are polite, which are more informal or colloquial and which forms they need to be careful about. In many lessons, informal forms are given first, then polite ones are given. Other lessons are arranged in other ways. As the teacher, you will need to give students some added information about the appropriateness of particular forms with particular people in particular situations until they develop the awareness of the language to do this by themselves.

(3) You should not try to work through the book sequentially, lesson by lesson. Rather, you should select certain lessons to work on using the Contents section as a check-list. Each lesson has the same format to help in selecting lessons as needed. However, since each lesson has the same format, you will need to vary the way you work with different lessons. You will find a number of suggested techniques and activities in the next section of this introduction, and detailed explanations of these techniques and activities in Appendix 2.

Using this Book

When you work on a lesson, I suggest you use the following four stages:

1 Reading
2 Discussion
3 Practice and Performance
4 Reflection

By using these four steps, you will make maximum use of students' learning time and energy.

1 Reading

After deciding on a particular lesson, ask students to read the Examples and Models sections before the next class. During the reading assignment, students have a chance to think and guess about the meanings and usages of various forms in the examples and models. These thoughts and guesses will be confirmed or refuted and revised in later stages. Some students find this step difficult at first because it involves thoughtful reading. However, it is necessary in order to help students develop the ability to understand and accurately guess about meaning and usage later, both inside and outside or after class.

2 Discussion

In class, then, you can read and discuss the Examples and Models with the students. First, read the examples aloud in a way which is appropriate to related imagined situations. Next, read the models aloud in a way appropriate to the given situations. The reading aloud is followed by discussion of the examples and models. In this discussion, you can touch upon a number of things:

(a) The meanings of words and expressions that students still have questions about,
(b) the context of the examples and models: the time, place, people and people's probable intentions and feelings,

(c) the politeness or informality with which things are said. Also, you will need to talk about which forms they need to be careful about and why.
(d) the intonation, stress and quality of voice with which things are probably said,
(e) what they themselves might think, feel, say and do in similar situations.

Discussions can range from teacher-guided ones to ones where students are working in their own groups with the teacher acting as consultant. You need to be careful not to belabor this stage, as students might begin to lose interest and enthusiasm. You need not talk about all the examples and models in great depth. Rather, you're aiming for understanding of major things: enough to allow them to practice and perform in the next stage.

3 Practice and Performance

This is the stage where students act upon their understandings. You can use some of the following techniques in practicing and performing the Examples, Models and Suggested Activities. (Detailed explanations are given in Appendix 2.)

Examples: Interpretative Reading; Skits/Improvised Role-Plays.
Models: Interpretative Reading; Talk and Listen; Puppet Shows; Tape Recording and VTR.
Suggested Activities: Skits/Improvised Role-Playing; Interpretative Reading, Questions on Papers; Values Clarification; Tape Recording and VTR.

An important thing in this stage is that students are on their feet and applying the things they understood and learned in the first two stages. They will need to discuss the situations in the "Suggested Activities" so they understand them. Their performance of the "Suggested Activities" is the "test" of their ability to recognize the need for and to use the conversation techniques and turning-points.

4 Reflection

This last stage gives students the chance to look back and comment on their experience. Some may still have questions; some may comment on the learning process and how they felt; some may have suggestions about how to do things differently. The reflection should help give a feeling of completeness, sharing and confidence so that people are ready to move on to the next lesson. With the next lesson, the four-stage process begins again.

General Suggestions

This four-stage process of reading, discussion, practice/performance and reflection should not be an overly-long and complicated thing. It will go slowly at first, but you will be able to go more quickly after students get used to it.

It might also help to keep the following suggestions in mind:
(1) Both you and the students will need a willingness to try something new and different. At first people may be shy, and things will be halting and confusing. The preliminary activities, which work on activity, instruction following and imagination, will help make everyone a little more comfortable about the process.

(2) Don't ask students to do something you yourself wouldn't do or something that goes against cultural norms. For example, don't ask Arab students to play roles involving heavy drinking. Doing so may cause conflicts with personal beliefs.
(3) In the practice and performance stages, help students to understand and act out the situation and people's thoughts and feelings by referring to their own experiences. Some of the preliminary activities in Appendix 1 work specifically on this.
(4) Don't go through the book sequentially lesson by lesson. Use the Contents as a way of selecting particular functions to work on. The students themselves can and should be consulted in deciding which ones to work on.

A note on usage

You will find in this text that I have taken some liberties that are rarely, if ever, seen in an ESL/EFL textbook. To reproduce that authentic colloquial speech of present-day Americans I have used the spelling conventions used by authors of fiction for this purpose. Thus, you will see some -*ing* forms given in examples of very informal speech functions with an apostrophe replacing the final g. In this same vein, you will occasionally see *you* written as *ya, What are you* . . . transcribed as *Wha'cha* . . ., and *Come on* as *C'mon.* For the most part, however, standard spelling has been used throughout the book. Also to reflect informal usage, the usual structural markers in Yes/No questions are deleted, as in *You catching a cold?* instead of the standard English *Are you catching a cold?*

Native speakers of English commonly use pause fillers or hesitation devices in their conversation. These have been transcribed, again adhering to practice in fiction, as *uhmmm* . . ., *hmmm* . . ., and *uh.* In addition, I have included meaningful sounds in their accepted transcriptions such as *shhh* and *yuck.*

Conversation Techniques 1

Ten Conversation Techniques

1 Opening and Closing a Conversation
2 Asking about/Expressing Opinions
3 Regulating Other People's Speech: Repetition/Speed/Volume
4 Asking for/Providing Meaning and Clarification
5 Reflection
6 Commentary
7 Interrupting
8 Checking Understanding/Clearing up Misunderstanding
9 The Topic of Conversation: Changing/Returning to/Preventing a Change/Avoiding
10 Bringing up an Idea/Adding Related Points

There are certain techniques that people use time and time again in conversations and discussions with other people. These techniques are used both consciously and unconsciously. Good conversationalists use them easily and smoothly. Becoming a good conversationalist in English involves, among other things, an ability to use these techniques. This chapter presents examples and models of language used in these techniques. There are also a number of suggested activities given in order to help you learn these techniques well.

1 Opening and Closing a Conversation

Opening a Conversation

A EXAMPLES (Read, Discuss and Practice)

There are many ways to open a conversation. The way you open a conversation depends on your relationship to the other person or people. Here are the four most common ways to open a conversation. Greetings are sometimes but not always given before them:

Greetings +
1 Introducing Yourself
2 Asking a Question
3 Making a Statement
4 Requesting Attention

The first way is generally used with strangers. The other three ways can be used with strangers, acquaintances or friends.

1 Introducing Yourself

You usually use this technique with people who you are meeting for the first time: at a party, meeting, public gathering, etc. It does not usually provide a topic, so it usually needs to be followed by one of the other techniques:

Hello. My name is Bob Stevens.
Hello. I'm Gary Justice. *I'm* a reporter for the *Daily News* . . . .
Hi. My name is Alison. *What's your name?*
Hi. I'm a friend of Ruth's. *My name is* Leslie. Leslie Smith.
Excuse me, haven't we met before? My name is Stanley. *You're* Alice Johnson, *aren't you?*
Pardon me, your name is Stella, *isn't it? I'm* Fred Hutchins.

2 Asking a Question

A second way to open and continue a conversation is by asking a question. You can ask for information, or you can ask for help. You need to be careful about the appropriateness of the question: especially personal questions. In addition, you will need to find a way to continue the conversation. Perhaps you can ask another question, or you can use one of the other techniques in this chapter.

Excuse me. How can I get to . . . ?
Pardon me, but is this the way to . . . ?
Excuse me, but do you have the time?
Pardon me . . . . Can I have that magazine when you're finished?
Where are you going?
Did you see the evening news last night?
How did you like the movie you went to see last night?

Are you still working on your book?
How did you do in the tennis tournament the other day?
My God! What happened to you?

Note: In general, people do not like personal questions from other people, unless they are close friends. Even close friends begin a personal question by saying:

If you don't mind my asking . . .
I know it's none of my business, but . . .
Can I ask you a personal question?
I don't want to be personal, but . . .
You don't have to answer this, but . . .

3 Making a Statement
A third way to open a conversation is by making a statement. This way can be used with strangers, acquaintances or friends in a variety of situations. Such statements are often related to the weather, to something the people talking see, hear or have experienced in common, or to the other person's appearance. Making statements is a good way to continue a conversation after it has started.

It sure is hot today, isn't it?
All this rain is really getting me down.
That's a beautiful view, isn't it?
That guy sure talks a lot, doesn't he?
That was a pretty interesting movie last night, don't you think?
I like that blouse of yours.
Mike! You got a haircut!

4 Requesting Attention
One last technique for opening a conversation is requesting attention. It is most often used if the other person appears busy, or is involved with something. It is also used when you have something special to talk about with the other person.

Hey, Doug. You got a minute?
Excuse me, Alice. Can I talk with you a minute?
Do you have a minute to talk with me?
May I have a few minutes of your time?
What I wanted to talk with you about is . . .
I've been wanting to talk with you about Mary getting married *for a long time now.*
What I'm calling about is . . .
The reason why I'm calling is . . .

B MODELS (Read, Discuss and Perform)

1 Two people meet for the first time at a mutual friend's party.

    P1: Hi. My name's Henry.
    P2: Hi. I'm Lisa.
    P1: This is a pretty nice party, isn't it.

P2: Yes. It is.
P1: Are you a friend of Bob and Sally?
P2: I'm mostly a friend of Sally's. We work together.
P1: Is that right. Then you must be a teacher too.

2 *Two office workers begin talking during break-time.*

OW1: Hi, Phil. How's it going today?
OW2: Oh, hi, Janet. Oh, so-so. I'm a little tired.
OW1: Really. Why is that? Didn't you sleep very well last night?
OW2: I slept O.K., but not enough. I began reading a book last night and I just couldn't put it down.
OW1: What book was that?
OW2: *Perjury,* by Mark Fillmore. Have you read it?

3 *Two acquaintances meet at the library.*

A1: Hello, Mary. How are you?
A2: John! What a surprise. I'm O.K. How about you?
A1: Oh, not bad. It sure is a lousy day today, isn't it?
A2: Can you believe this rain? I was getting so depressed at home that I just had to get out of the house.
A1: I know what you mean. Have you found any interesting books?
A2: Nothing really. How about you?

4 *A man approaches a woman at a party.*

M: Excuse me, Joan. Do you have a minute? There's something I need to talk with you about.
W: Sure. What is it?
M: It has to do with a farewell party we're planning for Jim and Kathy Mason. They're leaving the end of the month, as you know.
W: Yeah, I heard. I'm sorry to see them go. Is there something I can do?
M: As a matter of fact, there is. Can you . . .

CONVERSATION TECHNIQUES VOLUME 1

Closing a Conversation

A EXAMPLES (Read, Discuss and Practice)

There are a number of ways to close a conversation. Sometimes conversations end because no one has more to say. In such cases, people just become silent. Other times, one person may want to end a conversation. The three most common ways to close conversations are:

       1 Expressing Pleasure
       2 Making an Excuse   + Farewells
       3 Apologizing for Bothering

All three techniques are usually followed by farewells.

1 Expressing Pleasure

One way to close a conversation is to express pleasure at having talked with the other person. At the same time, you can express a desire to get together in the future. A definite time or place need not be set.

It's been nice talking with you.
I've really enjoyed talking with you.
This has been a really interesting conversation.
I'm glad we had a chance to talk.
You're really interesting to talk to.
I hope we get a chance to get together again sometime.
Let's try and get together again sometime soon.
How about getting together and talking again some other time.
I'm looking foward to meeting you again.

2 Making an Excuse

Another common way to close a conversation is to excuse yourself. It's not good to overuse this technique, or to excuse yourself for no real reason.

I'd like to talk with you some more about this, but . . .
You'll have to excuse me, but I have to meet someone at 4:00.
Well, I'd better be getting back to work . . . .
If you'll excuse me, I have to finish this report today . . . .
I'm sorry I can't talk a little more, but there's an important phone call I have to make . . . .
Can we continue this conversation another time? I have to get home and get ready for tonight . . . .
How about we talk about this some more, some other time. I really must be going . . . .

3 Apologizing for Bothering

One other common way to close a conversation is to apologize for bothering the other person. You can use this technique whether or not you really did interrupt or disturb him/her.

I'll let you get back to your work . . . .
I won't take any more of your time . . . .
I'm sorry to have taken so much of your time . . . .
I'm sorry for having taken you away from what you were doing . . . .
Well, I'll stop bothering you now . . . .
Sorry to have bothered you . . . .

B MODELS (Read, Discuss and Perform)

1 Two people have been talking at a party.

P1: . . . and so I've decided I'm never going to go back to that restaurant again . . . for as long as I live.
P2: Uhmmm. It sounds like you had a pretty bad experience.
P1: It was very unpleasant.
P2: Well, it seems like everyone's leaving. Maybe I'd better be going, too.
P1: Is it that late? I guess so. It's really been nice talking with you. I hope we get a chance to meet again sometime in the future . . . .
P2: So do I. And, good luck with your new life here in San Diego.
P1: Thank you. Bye.
P2: See you soon.

2 Two students are talking between classes.

S1: . . . I'm really sorry I can't make it this week-end, but I did promise my parents I'd be home. Thanks for the invitation, though.
S2: That's O.K. I hope you can make it some other time.
S1: Yeah. Me, too. *(Looking at watch)* Is it 12:15 already? Well, I'd better be heading for class, or else I'm going to be late . . . .
S2: Yeah. O.K. Well, take it easy, huh.
S1: You too, O.K.?

3 Two office workers are talking during break-time.

OW1: That's a really good idea. Thanks for the advice, Fred.
OW2: Don't mention it. I'm glad I could help.
OW1: And I'm sorry to have taken up so much of your time with my problem. I'll let you get back to work . . . .
OW2: It's quite O.K. What are friends for? Maybe we can get together some other time after work . . . .
OW1: Yeah. That's something to look forward to. And thanks again. See you later.
OW2: O.K. See you later.

C SUGGESTED ACTIVITIES

Opening a Conversation
1. You're at a party, and you see someone you want to meet. He/she is standing alone by a window looking outside.
2. You meet an old friend whom you haven't seen for a long time as you are leaving and he/she is entering the library.
3. A man and woman are at work. She's busy writing a report. He wants some information he needs for a report that he's writing.

Closing a Conversation
1. You're at a party, and you've been talking with a certain other person for a while. It's late, and you want to go home.
2. Two acquaintances are talking during a break in their hiking-club meeting. One is very bored and wants to escape.
3. You're taking a walk in your neighborhood. One of your neighbors is washing his/her car, and you have been talking for a few minutes. You want to continue on your way.

2 Asking about / Expressing Opinions

A EXAMPLES (Read, Discuss and Practice)

A second common conversation technique involves opinions.
   This technique is similar to "Asking a Question" and "Making a Statement" in Lesson 1. However, opinions are more personal than general questions and statements, so they are most often asked or expressed after the conversation has begun. As you know, some people express opinions freely, while other people are more reserved about them. In any case, everyone is usually serious about their opinions, and they want other people to take them seriously.

Asking Opinions
How was your trip?
How do you like your new car?
How did you find the lecture last night?
What do you think of Henry's idea?
How do you feel about this coming election?
Do you think that Miller's a good man to have as secretary?
Do you feel that men and women should have equal rights?
What are your thoughts on sex education for children?
What are your feelings about John and Joan getting married?
What is your opinion of the movie?
In your opinion, will this new program be successful?

Expressing Opinions
I found Morocco a fascinating country.
I think (that) Professor Martin spoke down to everyone.
I felt (that) there's wasn't enough cooperation among everyone.
In my opinion, it's a good idea.
As I see it, this program will never be successful.
As for me, I think this book is too difficult for most people.
If you ask me, I feel he has a lot of promise as a writer.

B MODELS (Read, Discuss and Perform)

1 Two friends meet just before class

   F1: I heard you went to see *Love Story* last night. What did you think of it?
   F2: I thought it was a pretty good movie. I enjoyed it.
   F1: Didn't you feel that the story was a little too simple?
   F2: Uhmmm, no. If you ask me, the simplicity of the story helped it a lot . . . .

2 Two office workers are talking during break-time.

   OW1: Tell me, Jim, how do you feel about this new no-smoking rule in the office?

OW2: Quite frankly, I think it's a good idea. As you know, I'm a pretty heavy smoker, and I have a feeling that it might help me cut down a little . . . .
OW1: Yeah. I can see that. As for me, though, I'm not sure I can go along with it.
OW2: Why is that?
OW1: I feel it's discriminative. There are a lot of other things that people do that bother me. If I have to live with them, they should learn to live with my smoking . . . .

3 *Two people begin talking during a club meeting.*

P1: Martha! Long time no see. How was your trip to Hong Kong?
P2: It was very nice, thank you. I found Hong Kong to be a very interesting place.
P1: Is that so. Where did you stay?
P2: In a hotel on Hong Kong Island. The Banyan Tree Hotel. Are you familiar with it?
P1: I think I've heard the name. How did you find it?
P2: In my opinion, everything was quite satisfactory, but there was nothing special about it.
P1: Well, I'm glad to see you back.
P2: I'm happy to be back. Traveling is nice, but, after all is said and done, there's no place like home.

C SUGGESTED ACTIVITIES (Read, Discuss and Perform)

(a) Improvised Role-Plays
1 You are talking about TV with an acquaintance at a party. You want to know what he/she thinks about a popular new TV program.
2 Two neighbors are talking in front of the apartment building where they live. One asks the other about his/her opinions about the changing neighborhood.
3 Two students are studying together in the school cafeteria. One student asks the other his/her opinion of the English class they study in.

(b) Discussion Practice

Work together with three or four other students or friends. Follow the instructions for activity (1) below. Then compare and discuss all your answers. Each person should try to help the others to talk about their answers. Then do the same for activities (2) and (3).

(1) Choose the most appropriate word describing you.

In your opinion, are you:

1 ...... more like the sun than the moon?
2 ...... more like the country than the city?
3 ...... more like a turtle than a rabbit?
4 ...... more old-fashioned than modern?
5 ...... more serious than fun-loving?
6 ...... more intellectual than emotional?

(2) For each of the following questions, give a 1, 2 or 3 to the three possible answers. 1 means "feel most strongly", 3 means "feel least strongly".

1 What is most important in a friendship?

...... honesty

...... generosity

...... understanding

2 What is important in a marriage partner?

...... a good personality

...... intelligence

...... sex appeal

3 Which do you generally prefer?

...... being alone

...... being with a few friends

...... being in a large group

4 What is the most difficult thing for you to do?

...... criticize a friend

...... keep a relationship with a friend who disappointed you

...... make new friends

5 What is money most important for?

    ...... living independently

    ...... helping to make other people happy

    ...... enjoying yourself

(3) Complete the following sentences.

1 On vacations I like to...

2 I get very angry when..

3 Talking with other people in English is.................................

4 Other people think I am..

5 The most important person in my life is................................

6 I think friends should always...

3 Regulating Other People's Speech: Repetition / Speed / Volume

Asking for Repetition and Repeating

A EXAMPLES (Read, Discuss and Practice)

Sometimes we don't hear or miss something that another person has said in a conversation. In such cases, it is necessary to ask them to repeat.

Asking for Repetition	Repeating
Huh?	*I said,* "I don't know where he went after the party."
What?	
Say what?	*I asked you,* "Will you open that door for the police?"
Say again.	
Excuse me.	*I said that* I didn't see him.
Pardon me.	*I asked* if you were ill.
I beg your pardon.	*I asked you* what time you're going to return home.
What did you say?	
What was that you said?	*What I said was that* I was too busy to go.
Please repeat that.	
Could you say that again, please?	
Would you mind repeating that?	

B MODELS (Read, Discuss and Perform)

1 *Two people are talking. One is not paying close attention.*

P1: ... and while I was shopping the other day, I saw this on sale and got it for half price. How do you like it?

P2: What? I'm sorry, but I was thinking about something else just now. What was that you just asked me?

P1: I was saying that I bought this blouse on sale, and I asked you how you like it. Is something the matter?

P2: No. Nothing's the matter. I'm O.K. . . . .

2 *Two friends are talking.*

F1: You'll never believe what I just heard.
F2: What did you just hear?
F1: Leslie won the $100,000 State Lottery.
F2: Say what?
F1: Leslie won $100,000 in the State Lottery.
F2: You're kidding.
F1: I told you you'd never believe me.

Speed and Volume

A EXAMPLES (Read, Discuss and Practice)

Sometimes other people speak too quickly or too softly and we can't understand or hear them. In such cases, we want to tell them to speak more slowly or loudly.

Speed
Please speak a little more slowly.
Could you please speak slowly.
Would you mind not speaking so quickly.
Slow down a little.
How about slowing down a little, O.K.?

Volume
I'm sorry, I can't hear you.
Please speak a little louder.
Could you please speak a little louder?
Would you mind speaking in a louder voice?
I can't hear a word you're saying.
Speak up, will you.

B MODELS (Read, Discuss and Perform)

1 Two friends are talking on a busy downtown street.

F1: I hear you're thinking about a new job.
F2: Yeah. I want to try doing something different for a change.
F1: What kind of job are you looking for?
F2: I'm . . .
F1: I'm sorry, I didn't hear you. What did you say?
F2: I said I'm looking for . . .
F1: I still can't hear you. Please speak a little louder.
F2: I said I'm looking for a job in Public Relations . . . .

2 A foreign student meets an American friend on campus.

FS: Hi, John. How are you?
AF: O.K. Celia. And you?
FS: Fine, thank you. Where are you going?
AF: I'm going to the gymnasium to play a little volley-ball with some friends. Do you want to come?
FS: I'm sorry, I didn't quite catch what you said. Could you please speak a little more slowly?
AF: Oh, sure. I said I'm going to the gymnasium to play volley-ball with some friends. Do you want to come?
FS: Hmmm. Maybe I will, if you don't mind . . . .

C SUGGESTED ACTIVITIES

What would you do in the following situations?

1 You're talking about your English class with a friend. In reality, your mind is someplace else, and you find you keep missing things that he/she has said.
2 Two college students are talking about their plans for the weekend. One always talks quickly, and the other always talks too softly.
3 You're asking someone for directions on a busy street. You sometimes can't hear what he/she's saying because of the traffic noise.

4 Asking for / Providing Meaning and Clarification

A EXAMPLES (Read, Discuss and Practice)

In a conversation, we sometimes do not understand either a word or something the other person has said. Or else, we sometimes want the other person to give an example or to explain something in more detail. When we do this, we try to improve the communication between us and others.

Asking for Meaning
What does baggy *mean?*
What is the meaning of estimate?
What is the definition of anticipate?
How do you define disorientation?

Providing Meanings
Baggy *means* loose-fitting.
The meaning of estimate *is* guess.
The definition of anticipate *is* expect *or* look forward to.
The dictionary defines disorientation *as* the loss of one's sense of direction.

Asking for Clarification
Huh?
Say what?
What was that you said?
What did you just say?
What do you mean by that remark?
What do you mean when you say he's a loser?
Do you mean that the shop is going to go out of business?
Does that mean that we can't see him yet, Doctor?
Is that to say that Dad's begun drinking heavily again?
Like what?
For example?
Can you give me an example?
I think an example would help me understand a little better.
Can you give me a few more details on that?
Would you mind explaining that in a little more detail?

Providing Clarification
I mean that I think you're being unfair.
What I mean by that *is that* he's never successful at what he does.
What I mean to say is that things don't look good for us.
What I mean when I say she's shy is that she never talks with anyone unless the other person begins the conversation.

For example . . . .
For instance . . . .
An example of this would be . . . .
O.K. Let me see if I can give you an example.
Here's an example . . . .
I'll try and explain that more fully . . . .
Let me give you a few more details on that . . . .
To give you some more details on that . . . .

B MODELS (Read, Discuss and Perform)

1 Two young women are talking about their previous evenings.

YW1: . . . and after the movie we went to his place to . . .
YW2: Huh? What did you say?
YW1: I said that we went to his place after the movie.
YW2: Oh, no. Tell me you didn't.
YW1: Why? What's wrong with that?
YW2: He didn't try any funny business while you were there?
YW1: What do you mean by funny business?
YW2: Well, I mean . . . he didn't try to get you to . . . uhm . . .
YW1: Oh, that. No, he didn't. He was a perfect gentleman . . . .

2 A foreign student is talking with an American friend.

AF: So, you've got a date with Luanne, huh?
FS: Yes. Tomorrow night. We're going to a party together.
AF: She's a really far-out person, isn't she.
FS: Did you say "far-out"? What does "far-out" mean?
AF: "Far-out" means . . . uhm . . . really unusual and interesting.
FS: I see. Yes. She certainly is unusual and interesting . . . .

3 A salesman is talking with an important customer.

    S: Bill Johnson was here the other day?
    C: Yeah. He stopped by with some new things he thought we'd be interested in.
    S: Huh. That's interesting. He's a real sad case, isn't he.
    C: What do you mean by "sad case"?
    S: Well, you know . . . . He's having trouble controlling his drinking again . . . and that company he's working for is having a lot of problems . . . .
    C: Is that so? Like what kinds of problems?
    S: Well, for example, they just can't get their deliveries to their customers on time . . .

4 A big-city mayor is being interviewed by a local TV news reporter.

    R: Mayor Boughs, the other day you said that the Atlas Chemical Company accident does not present a danger to local residents' life or health. Would you mind explaining that in a little more detail?
    M: Yes. I believe that no one was injured in the accident and that the chemical spill has been completely cleaned up. There is nothing to endanger the life or health of anyone living in that area or anyone living in this city.
    R: Does that mean that there will be no investigation of the accident?
    M: No, it doesn't. There will be an investigation.

C SUGGESTED ACTIVITIES

What would you probably do in the following situations?

1 You are talking with a friend from another country about festivals and holidays in his/her country. Your friend has a habit of using words from his/her own language, which you don't understand.
2 A young college student is talking with his/her professor. The professor is very proud of being educated and uses many long and difficult words. The college student tends to use a lot of slang.
3 You want to buy a new car, and you're talking with a friend who recently bought one. You are asking about the car, and he/she speaks in very general terms. You want more specific information, and you ask for examples and details.

5 Reflection

A. EXAMPLES (Read, Discuss and Practice)

Reflection is a technique where, like a mirror, you reflect back the same thoughts or feelings which the other person has expressed. We use reflection for a number of purposes. We sometimes use it to ask for clarification. We also use it to encourage the other person to continue talking. We can also use it when we want a few moments to pause and think. Lastly, we sometimes use reflection to help other people hear what we understood them to say.

There are two kinds of reflection: direct and interpretative. With direct reflection, we repeat almost the exact words the other person has used and make it into a question.

Direct Reflection
A: Jack and Jill are going to get married.
B: *Jack and Jill are going to get married?*
A: That's right. Can you believe it?

A: I told him to get out of my apartment.
B: *You told him to get out of your apartment?*
A: What else could I do? Otherwise, he'd stay all night.

In interpretative reflection, you give your understanding of what the other person has said.

Interpretative Reflection
A: Phil's just the perfect man for me. He's loving and sensitive. He's serious and hard-working. He understands me. I can trust him completely.
B: *You sound as if you're pretty happy.*
A: I am very happy.

The following expressions are generally used with interpretative reflection:

You sound as if . . .
You sound like . . .
You seem as if . . .
You seem to be . . .
You appear to be . . .
It sounds like . . .
It seems as if . . .
It would appear that . . .

CONVERSATION TECHNIQUES VOLUME I

B MODELS (Read, Discuss and Perform)

1 Two friends are talking after meeting at a grocery store.

F1: . . . Oh, by the way, Martha, did you hear about June?
F2: No. What happened?
F1: She's pregnant again.
F2: She's pregnant again?
F1: I just heard it from Laura.
F2: That's interesting. She's been wanting another child for quite sometime now, hasn't she.

2 A secretary is talking with her boss.

S: Here's the letter you wanted me to type, Mrs Brown.
B: Oh, thank you, Gail.
S: You're welcome. Is there anything else you want me to do?
B: Is there anything else I want you to do? Hmmm . . . . No. Nothing I can think of at this moment . . . .
S: O.K. I have some filing to do, so I'll get started on that. I'll be in the reception office if you need me.
B: Fine.

3 A teacher is talking with a foreign student after class.

T: How did you find the class this morning?
S: Hmmm . . . . To tell the truth, there were a lot of things I didn't understand. There were quite a few words I didn't know . . . .
T: It sounds like you were having a pretty hard time . . . .
S: Yes. It was pretty difficult. Maybe I shouldn't be in the class . . . .
T: You don't think you should be in the class?
S: Sometimes I begin to think that. Maybe I'm just not ready yet. What do you think?
T: My feeling is that you should give it a little more time. Today's was only the second class. You'll probably get used to the lectures and readings and discussion in class pretty soon. Your English seems to be good enough to handle it if you give it a try.
S: That sounds like pretty good advice, I guess. I'll stay . . . .

4 Two college room-mates are talking in their dormitory room.

R1: Hey! You got in pretty late last night, didn't you?
R2: Yeah. I guess it was about 2:00.
R1: So, how was your first big date with Linda?
R2: It was great. After the movie, we went over to that new jazz club on First Avenue. We sat and talked for a couple of hours about all kinds of things. She's really easy to talk with, and a really interesting person. We're going out again this coming Friday night.
R1: Hey, you sound as if you're in love, Frankie-boy.
R2: Yeah, well, this could be IT. I've finally met the woman of my dreams . . . .

C SUGGESTED ACTIVITIES

1 Bring a story to class. It can be about something that happened to you, or something that you heard or read about somewhere else. Sit in groups of four to five people. One person tells a story, and he/she stops from time to time while other people in the group reflect what he/she has said. After the story is finished, another person becomes the story-teller.

2 A college student comes to an appointment with his/her advisor. The student has some school and other problems to talk about with the advisor. The advisor knows the student pretty well and has found that reflection is the best way to help this particular student solve his/her problems. The student, after hearing the reflection, usually thinks of a solution to the problem him/herself.

6 Commentary

A EXAMPLES (Read, Discuss and Practice)

Facilitators are words or expressions that help to make a conversation smoother. They show that you are listening and encourage the other person to continue talking. However, people sometimes use facilitators when they're not really listening to what the other person is saying.

Uhmmm.
Uh-huh.
Really.
Is that so?
You don't say.
I see.
I know what you mean.

That sounds interesting.
That's nice.
That's true.
That's for sure.
Isn't that the truth?
That's too bad.

B MODELS (Read, Discuss and Perform)

1 Two high-school girls are talking on their way home.

G1: Guess what! Bob's coming home from school for the week-end.
G2: Really. That's great. What are you two going to do?
G1: Oh, I don't know. We haven't decided yet. He said, "Let's decide when I get there."
G2: I see. How long has it been since you last saw each other?
G1: It's been about six months now . . . .

2 Two retired men are talking at a senior citizens' home.

M1: My son came to visit me the other day.
M2: You don't say. What for?
M1: It was just his usual monthly visit. But he also invited me to stay the week-end with him and his family.
M2: That sounds nice. Are you going to go?
M1: Are you kidding? They have four kids. They always drive me crazy when I go there . . . .
M2: That's true. You always come back in pretty bad shape.
M1: Anyway, I've got a date this weekend.
M2: Is that so. With whom this time?
M1: Martha Hallenbeck.
M2: I see. A different woman each time, huh?
M1: You know the old saying, "Variety is the spice of life."

3 A husband and wife are talking in the living-room.

W: I went shopping this morning.
H: Uhmmm. *(Reading the newspaper)* That's nice. What did you buy?
W: I wanted to buy a couple of blouses, but I couldn't find anything I liked.

H: That's too bad.
W: I also tried looking for some shirts for you, but there were none on sale. Everything's so expensive these days.
H: I know what you mean. Food is expensive, isn't it.
W: Harold, are you listening to me?
H: Of course I am, dear. Did you see this article about . . . .

C SUGGESTED ACTIVITIES

Imagine you were in the following situations. What would you do?

1 Two secretaries are working in an office. The senior one likes to talk while working. The junior secretary wants to concentrate on her work, but doesn't want to offend the other.
2 You're talking with an acquaintance at a party. You're not really interested in the conversation, but you want to keep the conversation going anyway.
3 You're at a business convention, and you're talking with a business person from another company. He/she likes to talk a lot, and there are times when you don't have anything in particular you want to say but want to keep the conversation going.

CONVERSATION TECHNIQUES VOLUME 1

7 Interrupting

A. EXAMPLES (Read, Discuss and Practice)

Sometimes you want or need to interrupt a person you are talking with. Or, sometimes you need to break into other people's conversations. There are also times when you don't want people to interrupt.

Interrupting
Wait a minute . . .
Hold on a second . . .
Excuse me . . .
Pardon me . . .
Excuse me a moment . . .
Excuse me for interrupting . . .
I'm sorry to interrupt, but . . .
Can I interrupt you a moment?
May I interrupt a moment?
Can I break into this conversation a moment?

Responding to Interruptions
Yes?
Sure.
Of course.
Go ahead.
What is it?
What do you want to say?
O.K., but just let me finish.
Hold on a minute. Let me finish what I'm saying.
Just a minute. I want to say just one more thing.

Telling not to Interrupt
Don't interrupt.
Please don't interrupt me while I'm talking.
Will you please stop interrupting me.
Quit barging into our conversation, will you.

B MODELS (Read, Discuss and Perform)

1 A teenage boy is talking with his younger sister.

TB: . . . and what did you do with the letter after you read it?
YS: I was going to show it to Mom because . . .
TB: Wait a minute . . . . Does that mean you didn't show it to her?
YS: No, I didn't. I was going to show her, but I didn't get a chance to.
TB: Whew! That's a relief. Mom would kill me if she saw that letter.
YS: Why? What was in it that was so bad?

2 Members of a club executive committee are discussing dues.

M1: . . . and so, I think we're going to have to raise the membership dues again this year because . . .
M2: What! Raise the dues again this year? We've raised them every year since . . .
M3: Excuse me for interrupting, Martin, but we haven't raised them every year. We haven't for the past two years.
M1: And, don't forget, we still have the lowest dues in the area . . . .

23

3 *Two college students are talking when another approaches.*

    S1: ... so, I told Professor Wilkens that I just couldn't finish the paper by the end of the quarter.
    S2: Really. What did he say?
    S3: Hi, guys. Can I interrupt you a minute?
    S1: Sure, Phil, but just let me finish.... So he said that he had no other choice but to fail me.
    S2: He didn't, did he?
    S3: I'm sorry to interrupt, but it's important.
    S1: O.K. What is it, Chris?
    S3: You got a telephone call from Mr Grayson, your advisor. He wants to talk with you right now.
    S1: Uh-oh. I guess he's heard about it ....

4 *A young mother is talking with a friend when her son comes in.*

    F: Anyway, after last night, I think I'm in love with him.
    M: It sounds like you are. I hope things go well for you this ...
    S: *(Running into the room)* Mommy!
    M: Wait a minute, Pat. Don't interrupt. *(To friend)* Anyway, I hope things go well for you this time. You've had so ...
    S: Mommy, come quick ...
    M: Pat, will you please stop interrupting other people while they're talking. *(To friend)* It seems like you've had so many heartbreaks in the past. I really hope ...
    S: But, Mommy. Sandy fell down and hurt herself ....
    M: What? Why didn't you say so. Where is she? Is she badly hurt?

C SUGGESTED ACTIVITIES

What would you do in the following situations?

1 You're the host at a party, and you've just gotten a telephone call for one of your guests. The guest is in the middle of a conversation with another person.
2 You're at the office, and you're having a conversation with a colleague. Another colleague comes over and interrupts the conversation to talk with you about something different. You want to finish the first conversation.
3 A person calls a friend on the telephone for advice about a problem. Everytime the friend begins to talk, the person interrupts to say something else. The friend is becoming a little irritated.

8 Checking Understanding / Clearing up Misunderstanding

A EXAMPLES (Read, Discuss and Practice)

When people talk, there are sometimes problems of understanding and misunderstanding. For this reason, it is important for all of us to check our own understanding and the other person's understanding from time to time. It is also important to clear up misunderstandings before they become big problems.

Checking Your Own Understanding
Are you saying that . . .
Is what you're saying that . . .
Is that to say that . . .
Did I understand you to say that . . .
I'm not sure I follow you. Do you mean to say that . . .
Let me see if I understand what you said: you said that . . .
I'm not sure I understand what you just said. Did you say that . . .

Checking Other People's Understanding
Do you see what I mean?
Do you follow me?
Do you follow what I'm trying to say?
Do you get what I'm saying?
Was that clear?
Am I being very clear in what I'm saying?
Is what I'm saying clear enough?

Clearing Up Misunderstanding
I think I may have misunderstood you before. Did you say . . . ?
It seems that there has perhaps been a misunderstanding . . .
Perhaps we've misunderstood each other.
I think you may have misunderstood what I said.
Perhaps I didn't make myself very clear before.

B MODELS (Read, Discuss and Perform)

1 A manager and office clerk are talking on Tuesday morning.

    M: Good morning, Phil. How's the Harris report coming?
    C: Good morning, Mrs Taylor. The report's coming O.K. I should be finished with it by the end of the week.
    M: Oh, didn't I tell you? The meeting was moved up to this Thursday. It needs to be finished by then.
    C: What? Are you saying that I have to finish the report by the day after tomorrow?
    M: Sooner if you can. Think you can have it by tomorrow afternoon?

2 A stranger asks a woman for directions.

    S: Excuse me, can you tell me how to get to the library?
    W: Do you want the main library or the Goff Street branch?
    S: Oh, either one. The closest.
    W: O.K. Let's see . . . . You go five blocks down 1st Avenue here to the second traffic-light . . . that's Walker Street. Turn left onto Walker, and go about four blocks down the hill. You'll come to a bridge over the highway. Do you follow me so far?
    S: Yeah, I think so. Five blocks to Walker, turn left and go four blocks to the bridge.
    W: That's right. Cross over the bridge and continue on Walker until you come to . . .

3 A son is asking his father if he can borrow the car.

    S: Hey, Dad. Can I have the car now? I gotta meet the guys downtown in a little while.
    F: Have you finished your homework yet?
    S: Uhm . . . well, almost. I'll finish it later.
    F: No, you won't. You'll finish it before you go anywhere.
    S: Aw, Dad. I promised the guys . . . .
    F: Perhaps I didn't make myself very clear: no homework, no car.
    S: Aw, Dad. The guys will hate me if . . .

C SUGGESTED ACTIVITIES

How would you handle the following situations?

1 You're talking with a friend about his/her vacation plans. He/she says something about them that you find surprising. You want to check to see if you really understood him/her.
2 You're at a party, and an acquaintance asks you for a recipe that you make very well. You begin to explain it, but since it's a little difficult, you check to see if he/she understands it.
3 You're talking with a class-mate before class. During the last class, he asked you for a recommendation for a good restaurant in the area. You gave him one. He couldn't find it. You want to find out where the misunderstanding was.

9 The Topic of Conversation: Changing / Returning to / Preventing a Change / Avoiding

Changing and Returning to the Topic of Conversation

A EXAMPLES (Read, Discuss and Practice)

Sometimes when we're talking, we think of some different or interesting thing to say. In such cases, we may want to change the topic of conversation. Afterwards, we may want to return to the original topic.

Changing the Topic
Incidentally . . .
By the way . . .
To get off the subject a moment . . .
Not to change the subject, but . . .
That reminds me of something . . .
Do you mind if I change the subject a minute?
Can we talk about something else for a few minutes?

Returning to the Topic
Anyway . . .
In any case . . .
Getting back to . . .
As I was saying before . . .
Returning to what we were talking about before . . .
Let's get back to what we were talking about before . . .
How about we return to the subject of . . .
What were we talking about before? Oh, yeah. We were talking about . . .

B MODELS (Read, Discuss and Practice)

1 *Two friends meet during half-time at a football game.*

    F1: Did I tell you I got a letter from Bob last week?
    F2: No, you didn't. How is he?
    F1: Pretty good. He wrote he's going to Brazil this summer.
    F2: You don't say. That sounds interesting. By the way, did you hear that his old girlfriend is getting married?
    F1: Really? You mean Amy?
    F2: Yeah. To some guy she met at the beach last summer.
    F1: Huh. Is that so. Oh, well. Such is love. Anyway, Bob wrote that he hopes to stop by here before he leaves . . . .

2 Two company employees, a man and a woman, are talking in the office.

M: Listen, Sarah. How about going out together for dinner tonight?
W: Uhmmm. That sounds interesting. Where to?
M: How about that place that Greg Michaels always recommends — the seafood place on the water-front?
W: That's a good idea. I've been wanting to go there. That reminds me, I have to call Greg soon — about the party.
M: What party is that?
W: The one for Sally Jones — in the shipping department.
M: Oh, yeah. Her farewell party. Are you planning on going?
W: I wouldn't miss it for the world. How about you?
M: I'm planning on going, too. Well, in any case, shall we meet a little after 5:00? In the front lobby?
W: You're on. See you then.
M: See you at 5:00.

Preventing a Change of and Avoiding a Topic of Conversation

A EXAMPLES

Sometimes we're in a situation where another person wants to change the topic of conversation. How can we prevent a change if we don't want to change it? In addition, how can we avoid a topic if we don't want to talk about it?

Preventing a Change of Topic
Don't change the subject.
Let's not get off the subject.
Would you mind staying with the subject at hand?
I don't want to change the subject until we've finished talking about this one.
How about we try talking about that later. For now, let's continue talking about . . .
Before we begin talking about that, let's finish talking about . . .

Avoiding a Topic
Let's not talk about that.
Let's not bring that up.
I don't feel like talking about that.
I'd prefer not talking about that right now.
Let's talk about something else.
How about we change the subject.
Would you mind if I changed the subject?

B MODELS

1 Two friends are on their way home from a party.

F1: Mary. How could you do that to me? You embarrassed me in front of everyone.

F2: I'm sorry, Max.
F1: I've never been so humiliated in all my life.
F2: I said I'm sorry. What more do you want? Incidently, did you hear the rumor about Myron Daniels?
F1: Don't try to change the subject, Mary. I'll never forgive you for what you did to me.
F2: Oh, c'mon, Max. What's the big deal? All I did was make a little joke about you still living with your mother.
F1: Well, you had no right to bring my mother into the conversation.
F2: Oh, stop it. Anyway, I don't think it's right for a 36-year-old man to be taken care of by his mother like he's still a little boy . . . .

2 *A middle-aged husband and wife are having dinner at home.*

W: It's been a long time since we've heard anything from Billy, hasn't it.
H: Phyllis, let's not talk about Billy.
W: Why not? He's our son.
H: I don't feel like talking about him.
W: You never will forgive him, will you?
H: No, I will not. How can anyone forgive a son who takes the whole family savings and loses it?
W: Well, as I remember it, you were just as anxious to invest the money in that company as he was . . . .

C SUGGESTED ACTIVITIES

Sit in a group of four or five people. Each person has a small piece of paper and writes a question on it. Everyone folds his/her own card and places it in the center of the table or floor. Each person then draws a different piece of paper from their own. People then take turns answering the questions on the papers. Other people try to help the conversation continue.

Introduce the following variations:

1 One person changes the topic of conversation. A little later, another person tries to return it to the original topic.
2 One person tries to change the topic of conversation, but other people don't want to change it.
3 One person changes the topic of conversation and asks another person a question about the new topic. The other person wants to avoid the topic.

CONVERSATION TECHNIQUES VOLUME 1

10 Bringing up an Idea / Adding Related Points

A EXAMPLES (Read, Discuss and Practice)

When we're talking in a group of people, we sometimes have an idea that we want to bring up or something we want to add to the conversation. Here are some examples of ways to do this:

Bringing up an Idea
Hey! I just had an idea!
I just thought of something!
How's this for an idea?
What do you think of this idea?
Here's something we might want to think about.
Let me throw out an idea.
How does this sound?

Adding Related Points
Regarding . . .
Concerning . . .
In relation to . . .
I'd like to say something regarding . . .
Let me say something in relation to . . .
In addition . . .
I'd like to add something to . . .
May I add something to what's been said?
There's something else that needs to be said in relation to . . .

B MODELS (Read, Discuss and Perform)

1 Three students are talking about a friend.

   S1: . . . so it looks like Marty is going to be thrown out of school.
   S2: . . . we gotta try and do something to help him.
   S1: Yeah. But what?
   S3: I just had an idea.
   S2: What is it?
   S3: How about the three of us going to Dr. Benson and explaining why Marty was cheating on the test.
   S1: What makes you think that's going to help?

2 A group of people are talking during a club meeting.

   P1: Everyone knows their responsibilities for the picnic, don't they? Fred, you're in charge of refreshments.

P2: O.K. I'll take care of them.
P3: Excuse me. In relation to the refreshments, they ran out too soon at the last picnic.
P2: O.K. I'll remember to order more than the last time.
P4: I'd like to add one other thing.
P2: What's that?
P4: The last time all we had was soda. I think we should have other things too — like juices or something . . . .

3 *Three managers are discussing a company problem.*

M1: Well, moving on to the next item of business: we've been getting a lot of complaints about our salesmen pushing customers too hard.
M2: Have any names been mentioned?
M1: Not that I know of.
M3: Excuse me, but I'd like to say something in relation to that. It seems that most of the complaints are coming from our oldest and best customers.
M1: Is that so? That's interesting.
M3: In addition, two or three customers have done more than complain: they've dropped their accounts . . . .

C SUGGESTED ACTIVITIES

How would you handle the following situations?

1 You're with a group of class-mates. Your teacher's birthday is the same day as your next class. You're talking about doing something special. You have an idea to bring up.
2 A group of office workers are talking about how to make the office a more cheerful place to work. One person has an idea to bring up.
3 Three people are making plans to visit a nearby museum on the week-end. One person has been fairly quiet, but, at one point, wants to add his/her opinion to the discussion.

# Conversation Topics 2

CHAPTER 2

Fifteen Common Topics of Conversation

1. Weather
2. Sightseeing
3. Common Friends
4. Origins/Home/Family
5. Jobs and Work
6. Free-Time Hobbies/Interests
7. Past Experiences/Future Plans
8. Vacations/Travel
9. Education
10. Everyday Problems
11. Health and Illness
12. Pets
13. Food
14. Clothes and Accessories
15. Homes: Furniture and Decor

This chapter presents models of commonly talked about topics of conversation. From these models, you can get some insights into how people talk about these topics in everyday life. You will find that studying these conversations will be very helpful when you get into conversations with other people about these topics.

1 Weather

A MODELS (Read, Discuss and Perform)

1 Two people are talking on a viewpoint overlooking Niagara Falls.

   P1: It sure is a beautiful day, isn't it?

COMMUNICATING IN ENGLISH VOLUME 3

P2: It certainly is. The weather has been perfect for the past couple of days . . . sunny . . . and warm . . .
P1: It's been very pleasant. We've been lucky. I heard the weather report this morning, though. It said it's going to turn cloudy tomorrow. There's even a chance of rain.
P2: That so. I hope it stays like this for a couple more days, but maybe that's asking for too much. Is this your first time to Niagara Falls?
P1: No. I was here once before, a couple of years ago.

2 *A college student is talking with her father on the telephone.*

S: . . . so, how's the weather there lately, Dad?
F: Don't ask. We've had about two feet of snow the past couple of days. It's been really windy, too, so the snow is drifting a lot.
S: Is it snowing now?
F: Just a little. It's not as heavy as yesterday. We'll probably get another few inches, though. What's it like there?
S: Terrible. It's been raining for two days now. You can't go outside. It's depressing.
F: This has been a really miserable spring so far, hasn't it?

3 *A tourist begins talking with the waitress at the hotel restaurant.*

T: Whew! Today's a real scorcher, isn't it? Is it always this hot here?
W: No. Not always. This has been an unusually hot summer.
T: It's muggy, too. Do you think it's going to cool off any?
W: There's a chance of rain, which means it should cool off a little. When the weather's like this, we usually get thunder-showers.
T: Are they very bad?
W: No, they're generally not too bad . . . .

B SUGGESTED ACTIVITIES

How would you handle the following situations?

1 It is a really cold day. You meet a friend while shopping. Neither one of you likes the weather.
2 You live in a city that is famous for its rainy weather. A friend who is visiting you can't believe you're living there.
3 Two people are planning to go on a picnic together. One calls the other to talk about the weather.

2 Sightseeing

A MODELS (Read, Discuss and Perform)

1 Two sightseers begin talking at a Grand Canyon viewpoint.

SS1: Wow! Look at that! Now that's what I call deep!
SS2: It really is impressive, isn't it?
SS1: It's magnificent. I've never seen anything like this before.
SS2: Neither have I. This is our first time out West here . . . . My wife and I are on our way to California.
SS1: Is that so. My wife and I come from California. If you want to see another amazing sight, go to Death Valley.
SS2: We were thinking of doing that. Actually, we're on our way to visit my wife's family in San Francisco. A place I want to see is that park with the giant redwoods.
SS1: Sequoia State Park. It's also a fantastic place.

2 A young girl begins talking with a man on a plane to New Orleans.

YG: Is that the Mississippi River down there, do you know?
M: I think so.
YG: I never realized it was that big. Are you on your way to New Orleans too?
M: Yes, I am. I live there. How about you?
YG: I'm from Minneapolis. I'm going to visit my sister and brother-in-law in Houston. But I wanted to go through and stay in New Orleans to do some sightseeing first. Since you're a native, do you have any recommendations about places to see and things to do?
M: New Orleans is full of places to see and things to do. There are all kinds of tours to take, and there are a lot of good restaurants and shows. My wife and I are both very fond of the Latin Quarter.
YG: Really. The hotel where I'm staying is close to there . . . .

3 Two people are talking on a cross-country bus in the Rocky Mountains.

P1: The scenery here is incredible, isn't it?
P2: You're not kidding. I'm from the Midwest, so I've never seen mountains like these. It's all plains . . . flat as far as the eye can see.
P1: I know what you mean. I'm from Pennsylvania. We have hills there, but nothing like these. This is my first trip west, and I took the bus because I wanted to see the countryside on the way.
P2: Same for me. Where are you going?
P1: Portland, Oregon. How about you?

B SUGGESTED ACTIVITIES (Discuss and Perform)

What would you probably say in the following situations?

1 A visitor to your hometown stops and asks you for directions. You give the directions. The visitor then asks you about places to tour in the area.

2 A student is on a study tour of the U.S.A. The last part of the tour is a homestay with an American family. When the student meets the family, they begin asking him/her about his/her impressions of the U.S.A.
3 You are on a tour-bus in a city you are visiting. You want to strike up a conversation with the person sitting next to you.

3 Common Friends

A MODELS (Read, Discuss and Perform)

1 Two people meet for the first time at a party.

    P1: Hi. I don't think I know you. I'm Doug . . . Doug Holt.
    P2: My name's Mary Langston. Pleased to meet you.
    P1: Nice to meet you. Are you a friend of Bob and Sue's?
    P2: Sue and I went to school together. We were room-mates for a while. How do you know them?
    P1: I work with Bob.
    P2: O.K. Now I remember your name. He's mentioned it a few times.
    P1: Was it in relation to good or bad things? I'm just kidding. He's talked about you quite a bit, too.
    P2: Is that so? I think they're just fantastic people. I forget . . . . What do you do at the office?
    P1: I'm an assistant accountant . . . .

2 A young man is calling someone on the telephone.

    W: Hello.
    YM: Hello. Is Chris Levy there?
    W: Speaking.
    YM: Hi. My name's Steve Miller. You don't know me, but I'm a friend of Jim and Kathy Barton . . . . They're working in Mexico City now . . . . We were working at the same place for a while. They suggested that when I got to Dallas I should get in touch with you . . . .
    W: Jim and Kathy. How are they?
    YM: They're doing just fine. They really like the place where we were working, and they found a great place to live there.
    W: I'm glad to hear that. I haven't gotten a letter from them in months now. How about you? What are you doing in Dallas? What was your name again?
    YM: My name's Steve . . . Steve Miller. I'm just passing through on my way home. My home's in Nashville . . . .

3 Two businessmen meet in a bar during lunch at a convention.

    BM1: Hi. Mind if I sit here?
    BM2: No, sure. Go ahead.
    BM1: Bartender . . . a beer . . . draft. *(To the other man)* The name's Joe Franklin. I'm with Layton Business Machines.
    BM2: My name's Phil Jones, with Foster Industries. Glad to meet you. *(They shake hands)* Layton Business Machines, huh? I know a couple of people there. You know Terry Reese? In the engineering department?
    BM1: I know of him, but I've never really talked with him.
    BM2: Uh-huh. What department are you in?
    BM1: I'm in Personnel.

BM2: Then you must know Wally Johnson.
BM1: Sure. He's in the same office. He was supposed to be here, but couldn't make it. I'm filling in for him. You know Wally well?
BM2: Oh, yeah. We used to work together at GTB, back ten years ago or so . . . .

B SUGGESTED ACTIVITIES

How might the following situations be handled?

1 You're at a party, and you meet a person who attended the same college. You didn't know this person, but you want to find if you have any friends in common.
2 Two college students meet in a youth hostel dining-room in France. One goes to a college where the other has a lot of friends.
3 You're traveling around the country, and a friend gave you the name of a friend to contact when you got to a certain city.

COMMUNICATING IN ENGLISH VOLUME 3

4 Origins / Home / Family

A MODELS (Read, Discuss and Perform)

1 Two young people meet at a campground general store.

P1: Hi. My name's Dennis.
P2: I'm Judy.
P1: This is a pretty nice place, isn't it?
P2: As far as campgrounds go, I guess it's O.K.
P1: You don't sound as if you're very big on camping. Where are you from?
P2: I'm from Chicago. This is my first time, so I guess I'm not used to it yet. What about you. Where are you from?
P1: I live in Philadelphia now, but I grew up on a farm in Wyoming. That's still my home, I guess.
P2: Really. Does your family still live on the farm?
P1: My parents still do. Most of us kids have moved away, though.
P2: I still live with my parents. We're going camping for our vacation this year . . . . None of us really know what they're doing, but it's kind of fun . . . .

2 Two women begin talking in the lounge at a ski resort.

W1: Hi. Mind if I sit here for a little while?
W2: No, not at all. Here, let me move my papers.
W1: Thank you. Have you been here long?
W2: We arrived just yesterday. Al, my husband, is out skiing. I was out yesterday, but I'm a little tired now.
W1: Same with me. Oh, My name's Penny Murray.
W2: I'm Phyllis Gernik.
W1: Gernik . . . I've never heard that name before. What kind of name is it?
W2: Hungarian. My husband's family is originally from Hungary.
W1: Hmmm. That's interesting. Where do you live?
W2: We're from St Louis.
W1: Have any kids?
W2: Three. Two boys and a girl. They're staying with their grandparents this week.
W1: I wish we could have done that with ours.
W2: Are they here with you?
W1: Yes, they are. They're both out with my husband . . . .

3 A man begins talking with a woman on the phone.

W: Hello.
M: Hello? Is that Doris? This is Neal. Neal Lesley. Remember me?
W: Neal. Is that really you? I haven't heard from you in years. Where are you calling from?
M: From here in town. I'm here on business for a few days.
W: Really. That's wonderful. How are Sarah and the kids?

40

M: They're just fine. Sarah's got a part-time job now that both kids are in school. How's the family?
W: Jim's fine, and so is Margie. It's about to grow, though.
M: Really. You're going to have another? I remember back when both of you were saying you weren't going to have any kids.
W: I remember too. But things change, don't they.
M: I guess.
W: So, are you going to have any free time to come and visit with us while you're here . . . .

B SUGGESTED ACTIVITIES (Discuss and Perform)

If you were in the following situations, what would you do?

1 You're at a class reunion, and you meet a friend you haven't seen in years. Both of you want to find out about the other's family.
2 You're at a party, and you meet a person whom you're interested in. You want to find out a little about his/her family.
3 Two businessmen meet at a convention hotel bar. Both have had a little to drink, and they begin talking about families.

5 Jobs and Work

A MODELS (Read, Discuss and Perform)

1 Two recently-graduated college friends meet by chance on the street.

F1: Hi, Mark. How are you?
F2: Marilyn! What a surprise! I'm fine, thanks. How about you?
F1: I'm O.K. Did you hear? I found a job.
F2: That's great. What are you doing?
F1: I'm working in a bookstore downtown.
F2: I'm glad to hear that. How do you like it?
F1: I really like it a lot. It's a nice little place, and when things aren't too busy, I have time to read. It suits me. How's your job going?
F2: Oh, O.K. I guess. It's not quite what I expected.
F1: You're working at the telephone company, aren't you?
F2: Yeah. I'm in a management training program, but now all I'm doing is some busy work in one of the offices.
F1: It's part of the training, isn't it?
F2: Yeah. They say we need to learn about as many facets of the company as possible by direct experience, but, to tell you the truth, it's kind of boring.
F1: Well, be patient. Things just take time.
F2: Yeah, I guess. So, you're still living at home?

2 Two people, a man and a woman, are talking at a party.

M: . . . that's really interesting. How do you know so much about animals?
W: I work in a veterinarian's office.
M: Really. What do you do?
W: I'm an assistant. I didn't know very much about animals before I got the job, but I've learned a lot since I've been there. How about you? What kind of work do you do?
M: I'm a sales clerk at Murry's Department Store. It's only temporary, though. I'm going to school at night and studying computer programming. I need the money, though.
W: Computer programming is a field where there are openings everywhere. Do you know where you want to work after you finish school?
M: Not yet. But, as you say, it's a wide-open field, so I'm not worried about that. I notice your glass is empty. Would you like me to get you another drink?
W: Oh . . . O.K. I'll go with you . . . .

3 Two business people are talking on a flight to Chicago.

BP1: . . . so, have you ever been to Chicago before?
BP2: Oh, yeah. I've been to most of the major cities around the country a number of times. I average about four business trips a month.
BP1: Whew. That's a lot of traveling. What kind of business are you in?
BP2: I work for the government. I'm in the Department of Energy. I'm what they call the General Program Co-ordinator, so I meet with a lot of state and city officials and try to sell and implement new programs around the country.

BP1: That sounds pretty interesting. I wish I could travel more.
BP2: What do you do?
BP1: I'm an insurance salesman. I travel quite a bit in my local area, but it's not really travel, if you know what I mean.
BP2: Maybe. But at least you can go home at night. The travel part of my job was interesting at first, but now it's just really tiring. As a matter of fact, I wish I didn't have to travel as much.
BP1: I guess the grass always looks greener on the other side of the fence. You have a family?
BP2: Yeah. A wife and two kids . . . .

B SUGGESTED ACTIVITIES (Discuss and Perform)

How would you handle the following situations?

1 You're talking with someone for the first time at a party. You want to find out what he/she does.
2 Two old friends meet at a class reunion. They haven't seen each other for years. They want to find out what kind of work the other is doing.
3 Two college students are talking about their current part-time jobs and their job plans for the future.

6 Free-Time Hobbies / Interests

A MODELS (Read, Discuss and Perform)

1 An old member of a tennis club begins talking with a new member.

OM: Hi. You must have just joined the club . . . at least, I don't know you. Larry Holme's the name.
NM: Hi, Larry. I'm Mary Goodwin. I just joined last week.
OM: Well, I think you'll like it. It's a great place. Have you been playing tennis for very long?
NM: I used to play in college, but I haven't since then. It's been about five or six years now.
OM: Well, it'll come back to you. Do you play any other sports?
NM: I play golf now and then. I also play bridge, though that's not a sport, I guess.
OM: Well, you're in luck. Lots of people here play bridge. Does your husband play?
NM: I'm not married . . . yet. My fiancé does, though.
OM: Maybe we can get together and play sometime. My wife loves bridge. Well, I have to meet my partner over there. It looks like we're up next. Nice talking with you.
NM: It's been nice talking with you, too. See you again.

2 Two people waiting for a bus have begun talking.

P1: . . . so, imagine that, we live in the same apartment building but we've never met each other before.
P2: Well, it's a big building. Anyway, I'm usually never home very much.
P1: Uhm. What kinds of things do you do in your free time?
P2: I'm taking a couple of courses at the community college in the evenings. I also do some volunteer work at the city hospital two nights a week. Week-ends are my only real free time, and I usually visit friends.
P1: You sound busy. What kinds of classes are you taking?

P2: I'm taking one in pottery and one in sculpture.
P1: That's interesting. One of my hobbies is drawing.
P2: Is that so. What kind?
P1: Oh, just charcoals. Nothing very good.
P2: Well, I'd like to see some of your things some time. What other interests do you have?
P1: I'm into all kinds of games: card games, board games, and even TV games. I don't know why, but I enjoy them.
P2: Some are real fun. Well, it looks like our bus is coming . . . .

3 *Two students have begun talking at a theatre club workshop play.*

S1: Do you come to these workshop plays very often?
S2: No. This is only my second time. I have a lot of other interests that keep me pretty busy.
S1: Really. What kinds of things are you interested in?
S2: I'm a member of the sailing club, and go out sailing from time to time. I also belong to the hiking club. I also like to just sit and read or listen to music sometimes. What kinds of interests and hobbies do you have?
S1: Well, I'm involved in this theatre workshop program, and I've been in a couple of past productions. I'm also interested in dance . . . . I'm taking a modern dance class. I enjoy swimming, too. I like active things.
S2: It sounds that way . . . .

B SUGGESTED ACTIVITIES (Discuss and Perform)

What would you say and do in the following situations?

1 You're at a party talking with some other people. The conversation turns to people's hobbies and interests.
2 You're taking an evening music-appreciation class at a school in your area. You begin talking with another person in the class about free-time interests.
3 A radio interviewer is talking with a famous actor about his free-time interests.

COMMUNICATING IN ENGLISH VOLUME 3

7 Past Experiences / Future Plans

A MODELS (Read, Discuss and Perform)

1 Two college room-mates are talking in their apartment.

R1: Hey, Chris, have you ever been mountain climbing?
R2: Yeah. I went a couple of times a few years ago. Why do you ask?
R1: I'm planning on maybe going this week-end.
R2: Really. Where? With who?
R1: With Ted and Alice. They're thinking of going to White Mountain.
R2: Humh. Well, be careful. You've never been climbing before, have you?
R1: No. I don't know the first thing about it. Ted and Alice are pretty experienced, though, I guess. How did you like it when you went?
R2: I kind of enjoyed it, but I didn't like it enough to keep on wanting to. It's something everyone should try once in their life, I think. I remember the first time I went. We went to Mt Mirage . . . .

2 Two people are talking at a party.

P1: That's a nice necklace you have on. I've never seen one like it before. Where did you get it?
P2: I got it when I was in Alaska. I bought it from an old Eskimo who made them.
P1: You've been to Alaska? So have I. When were you there?
P2: About four years ago. How about you?
P1: I was there about ten years ago. I remember it as a really beautiful, unspoiled place, but that's probably changed by now. I'd like to go back sometime, though.
P2: I'm planning to go again this summer. Want to come along?
P1: Hmmm. That sounds interesting. I haven't made any vacation plans yet. When are you thinking of going and for how long?
P2: As things look now, I'll be leaving around the middle of June and staying for a month, maybe two . . . .

3 A husband and wife are talking at dinner.

H: Marge . . . . Do we have any plans for the week-end?
W: No. Nothing's come up yet. Why?
H: Mark Hamilton . . . at the office . . . invited us to his cabin in the mountains again. What do you think?
W: Hmmm. You remember what happened the last time we went, don't you?
H: Yeah. I remember. But this time we're not going to take any alcohol, so hopefully we won't have an accident on our way home this time.
W: Well . . . it's against my better judgement . . . but we have nothing better to do. When were you thinking of leaving?
H: The plan is to leave Friday night, right after work . . . .

B SUGGESTED ACTIVITIES (Discuss and Perform)

If you were in the following situations, what would you do?

1 You work in an office, and you hear that one of the other people in the office is leaving. You meet him/her during a break and want to find out what his/her plans are.
2 You meet a friend, whom you haven't seen for years, at a museum. The last time you saw him, he was leaving for a trip around the world. You want to find out about how it was.
3 You're at a party, and an acquaintance invites you to go sailing with her. You've never been sailing in your life.

COMMUNICATING IN ENGLISH VOLUME 3

8 Vacations / Travel

A MODELS (Read, Discuss and Perform)

1 Two office workers are talking during their break-time.

OW1: Say, Ed. Where are you going on your vacation this summer?

OW2: I haven't quite decided yet. I'm kind of thinking of taking a trip across the country. Mary and I have been wanting to for a couple of years now, but we've never had the time. This year I get a three week vacation, so . . . .

OW1: That's great. My brother and I made a trip like that a few years ago, and it was a lot of fun. Where are you thinking of going?

OW2: We're sort of planning on driving across the southern part of the country to California, then up to Washington State, and coming back across the northern states or Canada. What did you and your brother do?

OW1: We did pretty much the same thing when we went . . . .

2 Two neighbors are talking as they wash their cars.

N1: . . . yeah, well, that's a good idea. By the way, Jim, I've been meaning to ask you. Have you ever been to Spain?

N2: One time . . . about ten years ago, before I was married. I took a trip to Europe during one of my summer vacations in college. It's a nice country. Why do you ask?

N1: I might be going there for a two-week vacation this spring. I've never been abroad before, so I'm a little worried about what kind of problems I might have.

N2: Going abroad isn't that bad . . . . Especially if you go to a place where a lot of tourists go. Are you going on a tour or by yourself?

N1: That's the problem. I'm going by myself. I studied Spanish in high school, but I've forgotten most of it.

N2: That's O.K. Most places in large cities you can find someone who speaks English. In less touristy places — small towns and places like that — you might have some problems. But don't worry about it too much. You can always use sign language. When are you leaving?

N1: If I go, I'll be leaving in the middle of April and return at the end of the month. I can get a charter flight, so it won't be very expensive.

N2: And I think Spain is still a fairly cheap place to travel . . . .

3 Two married couples begin talking in a campground office.

H1: *(To his wife)* This seems to be a very nice place. The campsites are nice and clean . . .

H2: *(Overhearing)* It is a nice place. We've been here two nights. We've liked it. How long are you planning to stay?

W1: Two nights. We're on our way to the East Coast . . . Virginia . . . for our son's wedding.

W2: Well, congratulations. You must be very happy.

W1: We are. So far it's been a wonderful trip. We've seen a lot of nice things and met a lot of nice people.

H2: So have we. Camping is a very interesting way to travel.
H1: What are you folks doing?
H2: We're going west. We're thinking of moving to Arizona, so after we get there, we're going to look for a small house. We're really enjoying the trip, though, aren't we, Amanda?
W2: Yes, we are. It's been a nice trip. This is our first time camping, and it's been a pleasant surprise . . . .

B SUGGESTED ACTIVITIES (Discuss and Perform)

What would you say in the following situations?

1 You're talking with an acquaintance at a party. You begin talking about vacation plans.
2 You're a college student, and you meet a student from another country at a special lecture. You ask her what it's like to visit and study in another country.
3 A married couple are on their second honeymoon in a foreign country. They meet another couple from their own country while taking a tour of a famous museum.

COMMUNICATING IN ENGLISH VOLUME 3

9 Education

A MODELS (Read, Discuss and Perform)

1 Two people are talking at a party.

P1: . . . I thought it was a pretty good movie. Have you ever seen it?
P2: Oh, yeah. I remember when I was at Harvard, there was one movie theater that was showing it the whole four years I was there.
P1: Oh, you went to Harvard?
P2: That's right.
P1: What did you major in?
P2: I was in the history department. I was in African history.
P1: But you're working for IBM now, aren't you?
P2: Yeah. After I finished Harvard, I went on to a graduate program in Business Administration at Yale.
P1: I see. You've gone to some pretty good schools.
P2: Well, I had made up my mind when I was in high school: if I was going to go to college, why not go to the best . . . ?

2 A new office employee is talking with another young employee.

E1: So, how do you like the office?
E2: Oh, I'm really enjoying it here. It sure is a nice change from being in school.
E1: Yeah, I thought so too when I began working here. Where did you go to college?
E2: I went to Brightston College in Oregon. How about you?
E1: I graduated from Montana State. I started out in a community college in my hometown, but I wanted to continue, so I went to State. What was your major?
E2: Political Science. What was yours?
E1: Psychology . . . actually industrial psychology.
E2: I guess you had no problems finding a job, huh.
E1: Not really. I had a couple of offers, but this was the best . . . .

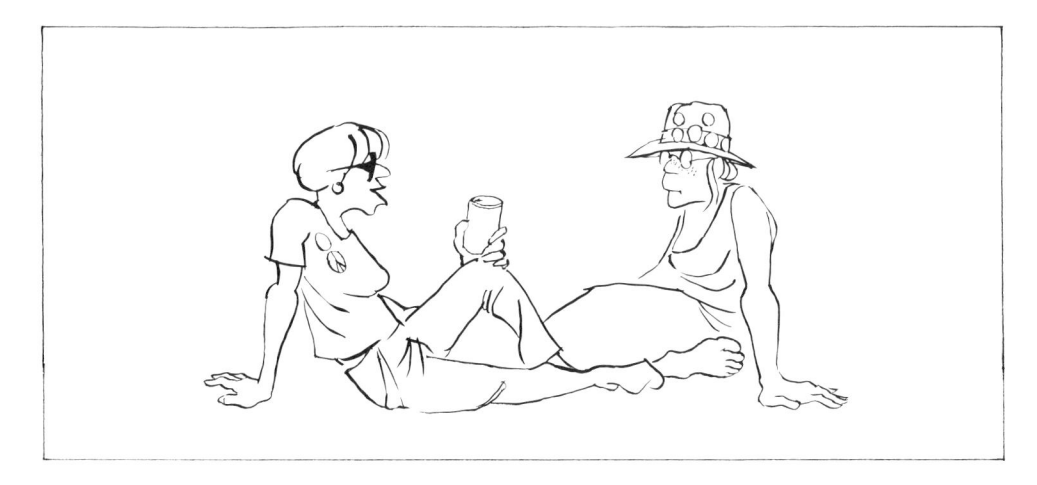

3 *Two college students are talking at a rock concert.*

S1: So . . . you go to school around here?
S2: Yeah. I go to Bronston College. How about you?
S1: I go to Hughes Business College. I'm taking secretarial courses there. What are you studying?
S2: I'm studying English Literature. It's kind of useless, but I find it pretty interesting, at least.
S1: What year are you in?
S2: I'm a sophomore. How about you?
S1: I finish this spring. After that, I'll probably look for a job somewhere.
S2: That shouldn't be too hard. I read somewhere that good secretaries have no trouble finding jobs nowadays.
S1: That's what I'm hoping. How do you like Bronston College?
S2: Oh, it's O.K. Sometimes I think about dropping out and working for a while to get some real experience, but I guess I'm actually too lazy to want to try . . . .

B SUGGESTED ACTIVITIES (Discuss and Perform)

How might the following situations be handled?

1 You're at a job interview, and the job interviewer is asking you some questions about your educational background.
2 Two college students who are traveling around Europe begin talking in the dinner-hall in the youth hostel where they're staying.
3 You're at a cocktail party, and the person you're talking to mentions that he went to college in a foreign country. You want to find out more about it.

10 Everyday Problems

A MODELS (Read, Discuss and Perform)

1 A party host greets two of his guests, a man and a woman, who have arrived late.

H: Gerry! Amanda! Glad you could make it!
M: Hi, Fred. Sorry to be late, but we got caught in traffic on the way here.
W: There was some kind of accident on the freeway, so traffic was backed up for miles.
H: Uhm. I know what it's like. I've gotten caught in the same kind of thing a few times on my way home from work. There's just so many people moving into the area that the roads are no longer adequate.
M: Yeah. And there seems to be a lot more accidents than ever before. People just don't drive as well as they used to.
W: We were cut off twice on the way. Can you imagine that?
H: Oh, well, you're here now. Try and forget about it. C'mon in the other room. How about a drink?
M: Yeah. I really need one . . . .

2 Two neighbors meet and begin talking in a supermarket.

N1: Hi, Fred. It's shopping day, huh?
N2: Oh, Hi, Leslie. Yeah, it is. But the way prices are nowadays, you just can't buy as much as you used to anymore.
N1: I know what you mean. It seems like things are going up a few more cents every week. Inflation's just killing our family budget.
N2: I don't know why the Government can't do more to keep prices down.
N1: I guess it's just too complex for anyone to be able to do anything about it. I'll tell you, though, I'm buying more and more sale items each week. You gotta try and save money somehow.
N2: Me, too. And I'm beginning to use coupons more and more.
N1: So am I. I never used to worry about it.
N2: So, how are things going for you otherwise?

3 Two friends meet and begin talking on the street.

F1: Hey Phil! How's it going?
F2: Oh, hi, Joanne.
F1: What's the matter? You look pretty down in the dumps.
F2: Oh, don't even ask.
F1: Oh, c'mon. Things can't be that bad, can they?
F2: They sure are. Everything that can go wrong is going wrong. I'm afraid I'm going to lose my job, I'm failing my night-school class, and Margaret's telling me she doesn't want to see me again until I get my life together.
F1: Hmmmm. It does sound pretty bad. Things will change, though. Most problems are just a matter of how you look at things.
F2: That's what my shrink keeps telling me.

F1: Sure. It's true. *(Looking at her watch)* I'm sorry, Phil, but I'm on my way to a dentist's appointment. How about we get together sometimes and talk about things.
F2: Yeah, sure. See you.
F1: Yeah. Hang in there, huh?

B SUGGESTED ACTIVITIES (Discuss and Perform)

How might you handle the following situations?

1 Your best friend calls you on the telephone. His/her voice sounds really unhappy. You want to help.
2 You're watching TV with a friend at your friend's house. You've been watching the news, and all the stories on the news have been bad news.
3 You're standing in line at the cashier's counter in a big department store. You're buying some household items. The person in back of you begins complaining about the prices of everything.

11 Health and Illness

A MODELS (Read, Discuss and Perform)

1 Two friends meet while walking in the park.

   F1: Joey. Long time no see.
   F2: Oh, hi, Lois.
   F1: How have you been?
   F2: All right. I had a pretty bad cold a few weeks ago, but I think I'm finally over it.
   F1: You got one too, huh? It seems like everyone I know has been coming down with a cold or something recently. I guess I'm lucky not having gotten it.
   F2: Yeah. How do you do it? You never get sick.
   F1: Right living, I guess. I'm also always really careful about my health. The way I see it, good health's one of the most important things you can have.
   F2: Hmmm, yeah, well, I guess I should try to take better care of my health. I really should stop smoking . . . and maybe try and lose a few pounds . . . .
   F1: You'll really be surprised at how good you feel if you do . . . .

2 Two office workers are talking during their morning break.

   OW1: Hi, Marge. How's it going?
   OW2: Hi, Bob. Not bad, I guess. How about you?
   OW1: O.K. Did you hear about Sally?
   OW2: No. What about her?
   OW1: She's sick again.
   OW2: Oh, no. What's it this time?
   OW1: She says it's the flu. Everyone in our part of the office is beginning to worry that they're going to get it now.
   OW2: You got to be kidding. I was working all day with her the day before yesterday. I don't want to get sick now . . . .
   OW1: I hope none of us gets it. Maybe you'd better take really good care of yourself for the next few days.
   OW2: I guess so. No staying out late; remember to eat well. I remember the last time I got hit with flu. It knocked me out for a month . . . .

3 A young man is talking with his mother on the telephone.

   YM: So. How's everyone at home?
   M: We're all just fine.
   YM: Are both you and Dad in good health?
   M: Of course. Your father's as strong as a horse, as usual. You know him. He's such a health nut, he never gets sick. I'm just fine, too.
   YM: How about Judy?
   M: Your sister's fine, too.
   YM: It must be the clean country living, huh?

M: Well, you know. We don't see that many people around where we live here, so we don't come into contact with many bugs to catch. Are you taking good care of yourself?
YM: Of course.
M: Are you still eating all that health food?
YM: Yeah, but not like before. I also eat meat now. You know, I was getting sick a lot when I was eating just the health food. So now I'm trying to eat more balanced foods . . . .

B SUGGESTED ACTIVITIES (Discuss and Perform)

What would you probably do and say in the following situations?

1 You're at a class reunion, and you meet a friend whom you haven't seen for years. He always used to look so thin and sickly. Now he's a picture of robust health.
2 You work in a small company. A number of other people have been coming down with bad colds and staying home. As you walk in, your boss asks you about your health.
3 You call a friend on the phone. Your friend answers and his/her voice sounds really soft and husky.

COMMUNICATING IN ENGLISH VOLUME 3

12 Pets

A MODELS (Read, Discuss and Perform)

1 Two people walking their dogs in the park stop to talk.

P1: What a cute little dog. What kind it it?
P2: A miniature poodle.
P1: Really. He's adorable. How old is he?
P2: He's about a year and a half old. How about yours? He's pretty big.
P1: Yeah. He is, isn't he? Bowser's five and a half now.
P2: So he's full grown. He must eat quite a lot, huh?
P1: Uhm. Feeding him gets to be a little expensive, but he's well worth it. He's a great guard dog.
P2: I can imagine. Well, we'd better get moving. Nice talking with you.
P1: Yeah. Same here.

2 A student is showing a friend some family pictures.

S: . . . and here are my parents again with my cat Neko.
F: Hmmm. It's a nice-looking cat. She looks like a Siamese.
S: That's what everyone says. We don't know. We just found her around the house when she was a kitten. She's nice to have around. You have any pets?
F: No. Not anymore. I used to have tropical fish, but I couldn't bring them to school here, and they all died, one by one, at home.
S: Oh, that's too bad.
F: Yeah. They were pretty interesting. But they weren't much fun as pets, though. I mean, you couldn't really play with them or anything like that.
S: Yeah, well, you can't really play with Neko anymore. You know cats. After they grow up, they become really independent.
F: That's true . . . .
S: I've been considering getting a puppy, but the apartment building where I live doesn't allow pets.
F: That's too bad. Where do you live?

3 A young woman is visiting a friend's home.

F: C'mon into the living-room.
YW: O.K. *(She sees a large bird cage)* Oh! What a nice bird cage. What kind of birds do you have?
F: Canaries. Their names are Marty and Morty.
YW: Marty and Morty?
F: Yeah. Marty's the female and Morty's the male. C'mon babies. Here's a little snack. Are you going to sing for us? No, I guess not. Do you like animals?
YW: I like most animals. I used to have a dog when I was young, but she died a few years ago. How long have you had Marty and Morty?

F: I've had them since I moved into this place. I guess it's almost two years now.
YW: Well, they're really nice.
F: They keep me company. So, How about something to drink? A cup of coffee?

B SUGGESTED ACTIVITIES (Discuss and Perform)

How might the following situations be handled?

1 You're visiting a friend's home, and your friend's dog comes and starts licking your hands. You're a little afraid of dogs.
2 You're taking your pet monkey for a walk in the park. A young man with his pet snake wrapped around his arm asks you about your monkey.
3 You go to a friend's house, and notice that they have a dog and a cat that seem to live peacefully with each other.

COMMUNICATING IN ENGLISH VOLUME 3

13 Food

A MODELS (Read, Discuss and Perform)

1 A young woman is visiting a friend's apartment.

    F: *(Opening the door)* Oh, Joan. Hi. C'mon in.
    YW: I'm sorry to just drop in on you, Larry, but I tried calling earlier to say I was going to be in the neighborhood and no one answered. Am I bothering you?
    F: No. Not at all. I just got back from shopping, and I was just making lunch. Care to join me?
    YW: Uhm . . . sure. Why not. If you have enough. What'cha havin'?
    F: Oh, just some junk food . . . a couple of hot dogs and potato chips and soda. I just have to throw a couple more hot dogs in the pot. I hope you don't mind.
    YW: No. That's fine. Is that what you eat everyday?
    F: Yeah, pretty much. I hate cooking, so I just make what's quick and easy and cheap. Food's not really that important for me, anyway.
    YW: Such is the life of the busy young bachelor, huh?
    F: Yeah. It's a tough life sometimes. So, what brings you to this part of town?

2 Three ofice workers are talking during a break.

    OW1: Hey, you guys, how about going out for lunch together.
    OW2: Sure. What do you think, Stan?
    OW3: Fine with me. What are you guys in the mood for?
    OW1: How about Mexican food. There's that new place that just opened down the street — the Mexico House. Interested in giving it a try?
    OW3: O.K. with me. I've heard that the food's pretty good there. How about you, Marge?
    OW2: Why not. What do they have?
    OW1: The usual. Tacos, Tostadas, Enchiladas . . . .
    OW2: O.K. Who was it that said the food was good?
    OW3: Bert Jones in accounting.
    OW2: Bert Jones? I've been out with him before. He'll say that anything's good. He's got no taste.

3 A young woman is being greeted by the host of a pot-luck party.

    H: Margaret! Glad you could make it.
    YW: I'm glad you invited me. Here's a little something for the party.
    H: O.K. What is it?
    YW: It's Eggplant Parmegian.
    H: Oh, really. Great. I remember the last time you made it. It was terrific. But, then, you're such a good cook that everything you make is terriffic.
    YW: Stop it, liar. I have a lot of failures, too.
    H: That may be true, but I've never tasted one. Let's put it on the table with the other things, O.K.?
    YW: O.K. But I made it this afternoon, so it'll have to be warmed up again before serving it.

H: Oh, O.K. In that case, let's take it out to the kitchen and put it in the oven a little while.
YW: Sure. I'll go with you . . . .

B SUGGESTED ACTIVITIES (Discuss and Perform)

If you were in the following situations, what would you do?

1 You're at an acquaintance's house for dinner. You're having some hors d'oeuvres before dinner. They're delicious, and you want to find out how to make them.
2 You're waiting for class to begin. A class-mate begins talking to you about food. He/she wants to know what kinds of food you like.
3 You're at a party, and you're talking with a person who just moved into the area about good restaurants in the area.

14 Clothes and Accessories

A MODELS (Read, Discuss and Perform)

1 A student comes up behind another student and starts talking.

S1: Wow! Who's that wearing that shirt?
S2: Huh? Oh, it's you, Marsha. Like it, huh?
S1: I must say . . . the colors are striking . . . to say the least.
S2: Well, you know. Clothes make the man and all that. I thought it was time to break out of my usual drab clothes and come up with something a little more colorful . . . like my personality.
S1: Oh. Is that how it is? Where did you get it?
S2: The shirt? It was on sale at an exclusive men's shop downtown. It only cost $28.00.
S1: Ah . . . huh. Only $28.00, huh? Well, it's . . . uhm . . . nice. So, where are you going?

2 Two women are talking at a party.

W1: That's really a beautiful necklace you have on. If you don't mind my asking, where did you get it?
W2: Thank you. My husband gave it to me for my birthday. The earrings go with it.
W1: They're beautiful too. They look like an Indian design.
W2: They're Navajo. He bought them on a business trip in New Mexico a couple of months ago.
W1: I see. He certainly has good taste. They look very nice on you. They also go very well with the blouse.
W2: I thought they would. I bought the blouse especially to go with them after he gave them to me.
W1: I wish my husband had as much good taste as yours.
W2: Harold has good taste, too, doesn't he?
W1: Are you kidding? He can't even match his tie to his suit. I have to do it for him. He never even gives a thought to clothes and accessories and things like that.
W2: But he's always so well-dressed.
W1: He wouldn't be, if I didn't take care of it for him . . . .

3 An office worker enters the office where colleagues are working.

C1: Hey, Frank. Is that a new suit you have on?
OW: Yeah. It is.
C2: Pretty classy. It looks really nice on you.
C1: Yeah. It really suits you.
OW: *(Smiling)* Thanks. I kind of like it.
C2: And are those new shoes, too?
OW: Well, you know. I had to get shoes to match the suit.
C1: What happened? Did you come into a lot of money?
OW: No. Northrops Men's Shop was having a big sale, and so I went and ended up buying a few things. Everything's forty per cent off.

C1: Forty per cent off, you say? Hmmm . . . maybe I'll have to stop by on my way home . . . .
C2: Yeah. Maybe I'll go with you . . . .
OW: You'd better hurry, before all the really good things are sold out . . . .

B SUGGESTED ACTIVITIES (Discuss and Perform)

If you were in the following situations, what would you do?

1 You're at a party, and you're really struck by a ring you notice someone's wearing. You ask about it.
2 A husband and wife are getting ready for a dinner party at a nice restaurant. They're both trying to decide what to wear.
3 A young man is giving his girlfriend a blouse for her birthday. When she opens the box and sees it, she knows she'll never wear it, but she doesn't want to hurt his feelings.

COMMUNICATING IN ENGLISH VOLUME 3

15 Homes: Furniture and Decor

A MODELS (Read, Discuss and Practice)

1 A young woman is visiting a friend's apartment.

YW: . . . this is a very nice place you have here, Stan.
F: Thank you. I've tried to make it look decent, and yet keep it comfortable and lived in.
YW: You seem to have succeeded. Those are some of the nicest prints I've ever seen. And is that a genuine Oriental rug?
F: Yes, it is. They make good investments, you know. I liked the design of it a lot, but the real reason I bought it was as an investment. That's why it's on the wall.
YW: Yeah, well, I guess you can't have people walking all over it with their dirty shoes on. I like the feel of the place, Stan. My compliments on your taste.
F: Why, thank you. Well, would you like something to drink? Coffee? Tea?

2 A party host is showing some guests around the house.

H: And here's the master bedroom.
G1: *(Going to the window)* You have a beautiful view of the lake from here, don't you.
H: Uhm. It's particularly nice when the sun sets in the evening.
G2: What kind of plant is this?
H: It's a Pteriolus, I think. I'm really not sure.
G2: All your plants are beautiful. How do you keep them so healthy?
H: To tell you the truth, I don't know. Susan takes care of the plants.
G1: That's a nice print over the bed. Who's it by?
H: A woman named Joyce Martin. She's not at all famous, but she does do really nice work, we thought.
G1: I agree.
G2: Is this a waterbed?
H: Yes. Care to try it?
G2: Uhmm . . . no. I get seasick on a waterbed.
H: That's too bad. C'mon. I'll take you to the guest rooms . . . .

3 A business person is visiting a colleague's home.

- **C:** *(Opening the door)* Hi, Joe. C'mon in.
- **BP:** Thanks. This is quite a nice house you have here, Harry. Is it new?
- **C:** It's a couple of years old now, but we bought it new.
- **BP:** It's very impressive. Do you take care of the lawn and everything outside by yourself?
- **C:** Yeah. I do most of it. Wendy takes care of the garden.
- **BP:** Well, you both keep it up very well.
- **C:** Thank you. It takes up quite a bit of time, but, for me at least, it's really relaxing work.
- **BP:** I can imagine. That's one of the problems with living in an apartment like I do. There's nothing to do outside.
- **C:** I guess, huh. C'mon into the living-room and have a seat . . . .

B SUGGESTED ACTIVITIES (Discuss and Perform)

What would you probably say in the following situations?

1 You're visiting a friend's home. He/she has made a lot of changes since the last time you saw it. There are some things you like more, some you like less.
2 Your Outdoors Club is having a meeting at a fellow member's cabin in the country. He's certainly put a lot of time and money into the place. You're impressed with it.
3 You're going to baby sit for a neighbor at your neighbor's house. It's the first time you've been in their house, and the wife is showing you around.

Situations 3

A. Relations with Other People
1 Greetings and Farewells
2 Introductions
3 Invitations
4 Entertaining Visitors/Visiting People
5 Dinner at Someone's Home

B. Necessities of Life
1 Information
2 Directions
3 Business Appointments/Reception Desk
4 Shopping
5 Restaurants
6 Doctor/Dentist/Hospital/Pharmacy
7 Services: Barber/Beauty Shop/Cleaners
8 Car: Gas/Service
9 Beggars/Salespeople/Solicitors/Proselytizers
10 Bargaining: Flea Markets/Garage Sales/Second-Hand Shops

C. Public Services
1 Telephone/Telegram
2 Emergencies: Medical/Fire/Police
3 Public Transportation: Bus and Taxi
4 Bank
5 Post Office

D. Travel
1 Travel Agency
2 Check-In/Ticket Counter
3 Hotels/Motels
4 Rental Cars

There are certain situations that we encounter again and again in our everyday lives. In each of these situations, there are some common turning points that usually come up as we play out the situation. Language related to these turning points is given in the Examples part of the following lessons. By becoming aware of these turning points, we can begin to handle these situations more easily and confidently. Of course, the turning points and situations may not go exactly as shown in the Examples and Models. However, by becoming aware of the possibilities ahead of time, we can be more ready to handle them when they do occur.

A – 1 Greetings and Farewells

A EXAMPLES (Read, Discuss and Practice)

Greetings

1 Hi, Larry.　　　　　　　　　　How's it going?
   Hey, Alice!　　　　　　　　　How're you doin'?
   Hello, Bob.　　　　　　　　　How are things with you?
   Good morning, Mr. Kim. + Long time no see.
   Good afternoon.　　　　　　　How are you?
   Good evening.

2 Fine, thanks.　　　　　　　　And how're you doin'?
   O.K.　　　　　　　　　　　　How about you?
   So-so.　　　　　　　　　　　And you?
   Not bad.　　　　　　　　+　And how are you?
   I'm fine, thank you.
   Very well, thank you.

Farewells

1 Bye. (Bye-bye).　　　　　　2 Bye.
   See you later.　　　　　　　　Hope so.
   See you again.　　　　　　　 Sure thing.
   Take it easy.　　　　　　　　 You, too.
   Take care of yourself.　　　　Goodbye.
   Goodbye.

B MODELS (Read, Discuss and Perform)

1 Two friends pass each other in the street.

   F1: Hey Jim. How's it going?
   F2: Oh, hi, Nancy. O.K. How're you doin'? Long time no see.
   F1: Yeah, it has been a long time. Too long. Unfortunately, I'm in kind of a rush right now . . . .
   F2: So am I. Catch you some other time, huh?
   F1: Yeah. Let's get together sometime. Take it easy.
   F2: You, too.

COMMUNICATING IN ENGLISH VOLUME 3

2 *Two acquaintances meet in a supermarket and stop to talk.*

A1: Hello, Stan. How have you been?
A2: Oh, hi, Luanne. Not bad, thank you. How about you?
A1: Pretty good. Today's shopping day, is it?
A2: Yeah. I have to buy a few things for dinner tonight.
A1: Uhmm . . . so do I. By the way, have you heard about Fred?

(A few minutes later)

A2: . . . that's really interesting about Fred. Well, I'd better finish my shopping. It's been really nice talking with you, Luanne.
A1: I've enjoyed it too. I hope we run into each other again.
A2: Yeah, I do too. Take care, O.K.?
A1: Yeah, you, too.

3 *A man wants to check some books out of the library. He speaks to the librarian.*

L: Good afternoon, Sir. Can I help you?
M: Good afternoon. I'd like to check out these books if I may.
L: Yes, of course. Here, I'll take them. May I see your library card?
M: Yes. Here it is . . . .
L: O.K., Sir. Here you are. These will be due the 31st of the month. Enjoy your reading, and have a nice day.
M: You, too.

C SUGGESTED ACTIVITIES (Discuss and Perform)

Imagine the following situations. What would you do?

1 You unexpectedly meet a friend in the drug store. You haven't seen each other for at least a couple of months.
2 A student meets his/her professor on the way to the library one afternoon.
3 Two office workers meet by the copy machine at work. They know each other only slightly.

A – 2 Introductions

Self-Introductions

A EXAMPLES (Read, Discuss and Practice)

1 *Hi. My name is* Eddie.
  Hi. I'm Liant. *What's your name?*
  Hello. My name is Paul, Paul Goodwin.
  I'd like to introduce myself. I'm Bob Peterman.
  May I introduce myself? My name is Ralph Winston.

2 *Nice to meet you.*   *My name is* Phyllis Ameryl.
  Pleased to meet you. *I'm* Connie Michaels.
  I'm glad to meet you.
  How do you do.

B MODELS (Read, Discuss and Perform)

1 *A man begins to talk with a woman at a party.*

   M: Hi. My name is Joshua Green. I saw you standing here alone, and I thought I might join you a moment.
   W: Hello, Mr. Green. It's nice to meet you. May name is Lori Stevens. Please call me Lori.
   M: O.K., Lori. Please call me Josh. Are you a friend of Dick and Tracy's?
   W: Yes, I am. I've known them for some ten years now. And you?

2 *Two married couples meet and begin talking at a campground.*

   H1: This sure is a beautiful lake, isn't it?
   H2: It sure is.
   H1: We just got here a couple of hours ago, and have been taking a drive around the lake. The countryside is also nice.
   H2: Is that so? We'll have to try that. By the way, My name's Harold Stevens. This is my wife, Rita.
   H1: Pleased to meet you. I'm Milton Westlake — call me Milt. My wife's name is Arlene.
   W1: How do you do.
   W2: Nice to meet you. Where are you folks from?

Introducing People to Other People

A EXAMPLES (Read, Discuss and Practice)

1 Henry, *this is* Alison Turnbull.
  Marge, *this is a good friend of mine,* Bob Jones.

Mary, *I'd like you to meet* Phil Sweet.
Lisa, *I'd like to introduce you to* Tom Martin.
Steve, *may I introduce you to* Ralph Butterman.

2 Glad to meet you.
   I'm happy to meet you, Bob.
   It's nice to meet you.
   It's a pleasure to meet you.
   How do you do, Mr. Butterman.

3 Nice to meet you, too.
   Same here.
   It's my pleasure.
   How do you do.

B MODELS (Read, Discuss and Perform)

1 *The host (H) and hostess (HS) at a party introduce two guests.*

    H: . . . so, if we move, it'll be next year. Hey, it looks like Ann is talking with Jill Martin. Do you know her?
    G: No, I'm afraid I don't.
    H: In that case, let me introduce you to each other. I think you'll like each other.

(They go to where Ann and Jill are talking)

    H: Excuse me, Ann. Edwin here says that he hasn't met Jill. I'd like to introduce them.
   HS: Oh, that's a good idea, Marvin.
    H: Jill, this is Edwin Needman. Edwin, I'd like you to meet Jill Martin. She's a friend of Ann's from college.
    G: How do you do, Jill. I'm happy to meet you.
    J: I'm pleased to meet you, too, Mr. Needman.
    G: Please call me Ed.
    J: O.K., Ed.
   HS: Jill works with the Public Health Service.
    G: Is that so. It sounds like interesting work . . . .

2 *Two businessmen are talking and one sees a friend.*

   B1: . . . so, business is looking pretty good. Hey, that's Martha Cowell over there. You know her, don't you?
   B2: No. I've never met her.
   B1: Well, then, let's go over and I'll introduce you.

(They go to where Martha is standing)

   B1: Martha! How're you doing? It's been a long time!
    M: George! What a surprise seeing you here.
   B1: Roger tells me you've never met. Martha, this is Roger Harmon. Roger, I'd like you to meet Martha Cowell.
   B2: How do you do, Ms. Cowell.
    M: It's nice to meet you, Mr. . . . I'm sorry, I didn't quite catch your name . . . .
   B2: Harmon. But please call me Roger.
    M: O.K. Roger. And call me Martha. What business are you in?
   B2: I'm with Lightship Industries. We make gliders.
   B1: Martha's with Control Systems, Inc. As you know, they make aerospace guidance systems . . . .
   B2: I know. What part of the company are you in, Martha?

C SUGGESTED ACTIVITIES (Discuss and Perform)

How could the following situations be handled?

1 You are a member of a hobby club, and your club is having a membership drive. You are at an open house, and you see some people come in. You want to interest them in the club.
2 You're walking down the street with your parents, and you see an acquaintance approaching from the other direction.
3 A businessman and businesswoman are having lunch at a restaurant. She sees a colleague come in and wants to introduce the man to her colleague.

COMMUNICATING IN ENGLISH VOLUME 3

A – 3 Invitations

A EXAMPLES (Read, Discuss and Practice)

Would you like to come with me to the beach this week-end?
I was wondering if you would be interested in going bowling tonight?
How would you like to come to a small get-together at Bob's house?
I'd like to invite you to a farewell party for John on Sunday.
May I invite you to my house for dinner tomorrow evening?
How about going out for lunch together this afternoon?
Would you be interested in going to the new exhibition at the museum?
What do you say we go to a movie tonight?
Why don't you stop by the house sometime soon?
Please feel free to drop by my place anytime.

Accepting
Thank you. I'll be happy to come.
That's very kind of you.
I'd love to go with you.
That sounds wonderful.
Thank you for your invitation.
I'll be glad to come.
I accept your invitation.
I'm looking foward to it.

Declining
I'm sorry, I'm afraid I can't.
I'm sorry to say I can't.
I'd love to, but I can't.
Thank you for your invitation, but I don't think I can make it.
Unfortunately, I'm already busy that evening.
I'm sorry, but I have a prior engagement for that evening.

B MODELS (Read, Discuss and Perform)

1 *Two women are talking on the telephone.*

W1: . . . I'm glad to hear that everyone's fine. By the way, the main reason I called is that Pete and I want to have a small party for Al and Mary before they leave for Europe this Saturday. The party will be Friday evening, after dinner. We were wondering if you and Mark would be interested in coming?

W2: That sounds wonderful. I don't think we have plans for that evening. Just let me ask Mark, O.K.?

W1: Of course. I'll hold.

(A minute later)

W2: Hello, June? We're free that evening. We'd love to come.
W1: Wonderful. The party will start around 8:00.
W2: Is there anything we can bring?
W1: I think we'll have plenty. But, if there's something special you want to bring . . . .
W2: O.K. I'll probably think of something . . . .

2 *Two teachers are talking during a mid-morning break.*

T1: Hey, Tom. What do you say we go out for lunch together today? My treat.

T2: I'm sorry, Bill, but I've already made plans to go out with Debby. How would you like to come with us?
T1: Where are you thinking of going?
T2: Just to that sandwich shop down the street.
T1: That sounds pretty good. I will join you, if you don't mind.
T2: Not at all. We're leaving right after class. Let's meet out front.
T1: O.K. See you there. Thanks.

3 *A student begins talking with another student.*

S1: Hey, Jerry. Wait up a minute . . . .
S2: Oh, Hi, Herb. What's up?
S1: There's something I want to ask you. As you know, I'm a member of the Bible Study Group on campus, and we're going to have an open house for new members this Sunday. I'd like to invite you to come, if you want . . . .
S2: Hmmm, I'm sorry, Herb, but I'm afraid I can't. I've already made other plans. Thank you for the invitation, though.
S1: O.K. Well, maybe some other time. I think you'd like . . .

C SUGGESTED ACTIVITIES (Discuss and Perform)

What would you do in the following situations?

1 You're going to have a party at your apartment. You meet a friend, who you want to invite, by chance at the supermarket.
2 A colleague in your office invites you out for dinner. You accept.
3 An acquaintance invites you to a party. You don't want to go.

A – 4 Entertaining Visitors / Visiting People

A EXAMPLES (Read, Discuss and Practice)

Host/Hostess
Come in.
C'mon in.
Let me take your coat.
Here. I'll take your things.
Make yourself at home.
Make yourself comfortable.
Our home is your home.
Here. Have a seat.
Please sit down.
Why don't you sit here.
Would you like a drink?
Would you like something to drink?
How about a cup of coffee?
Help yourself to the things on the table.
Here. Have some cake.
Try some butter cookies.
Is there anything I can get you?
Is there anything you want?
Can I get you something?
Thank you for coming.
Thanks for stopping by.
You'll have to come again sometime soon.
Please feel free to drop by anytime.
It's been our pleasure.

Visitor
Thank you.
Thank you for inviting me.
You have a very nice place.
What a nice place this is.
Would you mind if I smoked?
Is it O.K. if I smoke?
May I smoke?
Maybe I'll have a gin and tonic.
Nothing now. Maybe I'll have something a little later.
No, thank you.
Can I have a glass of water?
Is it possible to have a cup of tea?
Excuse me, Mary. Where is your bathroom.
Can you tell me where the bathroom is?
I should be going . . . .
It's time for me to be going . . . .
We've got to be going pretty soon . . . .
Thank you for inviting us.
Thank you for having us over.
We'll have to have you come to our place sometime soon.
I've had a wonderful time.
This has been a very nice evening.
I really enjoyed myself tonight.

B MODELS (Read, Discuss and Perform)

1 A businessman is visiting the home of an associate for the first time.

A: *(Opening the door)* Ted. Good to see you. Come in. Did you have any trouble finding our place?
B: Thank you. No, no trouble. Your instructions were fine.
A: Is it still raining?
B: Just a little. Not as bad as before.
A: Here, let me take your things. Go on into the living-room. I'll be with you in a minute.
B: O.K.

(The visitor enters the living-room and meets the associate's wife)

W: Hello. You must be Ted. Steve's told me a lot about you. My name's Elizabeth.
B: I'm happy to meet you, Elizabeth. I've heard a lot about you.
A: *(Entering)* So, you two have met already?
B: Yes, we have.
A: Well, make yourself at home, Ted. Why don't you sit here. Would you like a drink?
B: Yes, I would, thank you.
A: What's your pleasure?
B: Maybe I'll have a scotch and water, if you have it . . . .
A: Of course. Coming right up.
W: Help yourself to some of the things on the table. The green dip is avocado, and the white is onion.
B: Thank you. I'll try some. The cake looks good, too.
W: Believe it or not, Steve made it.
B: Is that so. I'll have to have some.
A: *(Returning)* Here's your drink, Ted. I hope it's O.K. So, how long will you be in New York this trip?
B: About two weeks. I was sent to . . . .

(Later in the evening)

B: . . . It sounds like you had a nice time in Mexico. By the way, could you tell me where your bathroom is?
A: Of course. It's upstairs, right at the top of the stairs.
B: Thanks. I'll be back in a minute.

(The visitor decides it's time to go home)

B: . . . Well, it looks like it's getting a little late. I think I'd better be going . . . .
W: So soon? Can't you stay a little longer?
B: I'd really like to, but I've got quite a busy day tomorrow . . . .
A: Both of us do, don't we. Well, let me get your things.

B: Thanks. And thank you for having me over this evening. I really enjoyed myself.
W: It's been our pleasure. I hope we have a chance to meet again.
B: So do I. Well, see you tomorrow, Steve.
A: Yep. Tomorrow morning. Thanks for coming by.
W: Goodbye, Ted.
A: See you again, Elizabeth.

C SUGGESTED ACTIVITIES (Discuss and Perform)

How would you handle the following situations?

1 A friend who you have invited to your house has just arrived.
2 You're visiting an acquaintance's house and want to smoke, but you see no ashtrays.
3 You're at a party at a colleague's house, and you want to use the bathroom. You're not sure where it is.
4 You had dinner at an acquaintance's house, and it's gotten late and you want to return home.

A – 5 Dinner at Someone's Home

A EXAMPLES (Read, Discuss and Practice)

Host/Hostess
Dinner is ready.
Dinner's on the table.
Why don't we all sit down at the table?
Here. Please sit here.
Have a seat, here.
Why don't you sit next to . . . .
Here, have some vegetables.
Here, help yourself to some mashed potatoes.
Try some of this garlic bread.
Would you like some cheese?
How about some more corn?
Would you like some more peas?
Help yourself to seconds.
Have seconds on the turkey.
You sure you won't have any more?
Is that all you're going to eat?
Save some room for dessert.
Would you like coffee or tea?

Visitor
Everything looks delicious.
Everything looks so good.
Could you please pass the salt?
Could I have the gravy, *please?*
Can you pass me the potatoes?
Can I have some more water?
Is there any more rice?
I think I'll have seconds on the roast beef.
Would you mind if I had seconds on the cauliflower?
No, thank you. I'm full.
I'm quite full, thank you.
I've eaten more than enough already, thank you.
I couldn't eat another thing.
Everything was delicious.
That was a great meal.
I've never had such a good meal.
Coffee, please.
I'll have tea, if it's no trouble.

B MODELS (Read, Discuss and Perform)

1 A young woman brings a foreign student friend to her mother's and father's home for dinner. They are talking in the living-room.

M: *(Entering)* Excuse me, everyone. Dinner's on the table.
F: Well, let's begin before it gets cold. C'mon in to the dining-room, Maria.
FS: Thank you.

(In the dining-room)

M: Henry, why don't you sit at your usual place at the head of the table. Maria, you sit here, on this side. Alice, you sit in your usual place. I'll sit here, near the kitchen.
FS: Everything looks delicious, Mrs. Spence.
YW: Yeah, Mom. It looks great.
M: Thank you. Henry, why don't you begin the vegetables. Maria, help yourself to the roast beef. Don't be shy. Take as much as you want. Everyone in this family is a big eater.
FS: Thank you. I'll just take a little for now, though.
M: The rare pieces are on the side, and the well-done on that side. Have some gravy with it, too. Alice, why don't you start the potatoes. I'll have a roll.
YW: O.K. Mom.

F: Maria, is that all the meat you're going to have? Take a little more. Here, have some eggplant, too.
FS: Uhm, no thank you. I've never been able to eat eggplant . . . .
YW: Is that so. I'm sorry, I didn't know. All of us have some things we don't like, though. I understand.
YW: Mom. May I have a roll, please?
M: O.K. Would you like a roll, too, Maria.
FS: Yes, I would, thank you.
F: Margaret, Maria says that she's going to be studying in the States for about four or five years . . . .
M: Is that so? What are you going to study?

(Later)

F: Maria. Your plate is almost empty. Help yourself to seconds.
FS: Thank you, Mr. Spence, but I'm almost full.
M: How about just a little more roast beef?
FS: Well, maybe just one more small piece . . . .
YW: Mom, could you please pass the butter?
M: Of course. Here you are.
F: Margaret, could I have another glass of water.
M: O.K. Here you are. Maria, is there anything else you want?
FS: No, thank you. I've eaten too much already.
F: Save a little room for dessert. Margaret made a peach pie just for you.
FS: Thank you, Mrs. Spence. Everything's been so good.
F: What's your favorite food in your country, Maria?

(Near the end of dinner)

F: Well, Margaret, it seems as if everyone's finished.
YW: Do you want some help clearing the table, Mom?
FS: Yes. May I help too?
M: No, thank you. Both of you just sit here. I can handle it myself. Would everyone like dessert now or later?
F: I think everyone is pretty full. Maybe later. How about you, Maria?
FS: Later would be fine with me. I couldn't eat another thing now.
M: O.K. Why don't all of you just go and sit and relax in the other room. I'll take care of the table. But first, who will want coffee and who tea?
F: Coffee.
YW: Tea for me, Mom.
M: And you, Maria?
FS: Tea, please.
M: O.K. Two coffees and two teas. I'll bring everything a little later.
FS: Thank you, Mrs. Spence. This has been a delicious meal.
M: Thank you, Maria. I'm glad you enjoyed it.
F: Well, you two, let's go sit down in the living-room . . . .

C SUGGESTED ACTIVITIES (Discuss and Perform)

What would you say and do in the following situations?

1 You have some guests for dinner. They are sitting and talking in the living-room. You call them to the table to sit down.

2 You want your guests to begin taking food.
3 You're having dinner at an acquaintance's house. He/she offers the spinach. You hate spinach.
4 You've eaten as much as you can, and the hostess offers you some more.

B – 1 Information

A EXAMPLES (Read, Discuss and Practice)

Can you help me?
Can you tell me what time United Flight 98 arrives from Portland?
Do you know where the sporting-goods section is?
Can you give me some information about bus tours in the city?
I'd like some information about the water heater you have on sale.
I'd like to find out about part-time sales jobs you have.
I'm calling for information about the ad. you have in the newspaper.

B MODELS (Read, Discuss and Perform)

1 A woman is calling the city bus terminal for information. She speaks to a clerk.

   C: Hello. City Bus Terminal.
   W: Yes. Can you tell me what time the bus from Los Angeles arrives? I have to meet someone on the bus.
   C: We have two busses arriving from Los Angeles. One is at 2:30 and one at 4:15. Do you know which one it is?
   W: It's the one that left Los Angeles at 7:30 this morning.
   C: That's the 2:30 bus.
   W: Is it on time?
   C: It's on time.
   W: Thank you.
   C: You're welcome.

2 A man stops at his hotel's tour information center. He speaks to a clerk.

   M: Good morning. Can you help me? I'd like some information about tours I can take in and around the city.
   C: Yes Sir. What kinds of tours are you interested in, walking tours, bus tours or special limousine tours?
   M: I'm not sure. I'd like information about a number of different kinds of tours available.
   C: O.K., Sir. Here are some brochures describing tours in the city. Why don't you have a look at these, and if you have any questions or want to make arrangements, I'll be glad to help you.
   M: O.K. Let me have a look at these. Thanks.
   C: You're welcome.

3 Two men are talking about a newspaper classified advertisement.

   M1: Hello.
   M2: Hello. I'm calling for more information about the '79 Datsun hatchback you have advertised in the newspaper.
   M1: O.K. What can I tell you about it?
   M2: Well, I have several questions. One is, how many miles does it have on it?

4 A woman is looking at a camera in a camera shop. She speaks to a shop assistant.

   SA: Can I help you, Miss?
   W: Yes. I'm interested in this camera, but I'd like to have some more information about it first.
   SA: Of course. What question do you have about it?
   W: Well, first, how long is the warranty on it?

5 A student enters his college's business-department office. He speaks to a secretary.

   S: Hi. Is there something I can do for you?
   ST: Hi. Yes. I'd like to find out about majoring in business.
   S: I see. Well, I can give you some information about it and perhaps answer some of your questions. Dr. Browning is the department advisor, and he could help you a lot more. What kinds of things would you like to know?
   ST: One of my questions is: how many credits do I need to take?

C SUGGESTED ACTIVITIES

How might the following situations be handled?

1 It's late Sunday afternoon, and you need to buy something at a certain store. You're not sure what time it closes.
2 You're new in town and you're looking for an apartment. You see an ad. in the paper for a 2BR apartment for $325. You want to get more information about it.
3 You're in a department store, and you want to buy a watch. You see one you like, and want more information about it.

COMMUNICATING IN ENGLISH VOLUME 3

B – 2 Directions

A EXAMPLES (Read, Discuss and Practice)

Asking for Directions
I'm looking for the City Art Museum.
I'm trying to get to the downtown bus terminal.
Can you tell me how to get to the waterfront from here?
Do you know where the IBM building is?
Is this the way to Hideaway Park?
Do you know how to get to Martinsville from here?
How can I get to the airport from here?

Giving Directions
Go up 1st Avenue *to* . . .
Go down Jackson Avenue *five blocks to* Mercer Street.
Turn right on 45th Street N.E.
Make a left onto Broadway.
Continue on Badern *until you come to the second stop-light.*
Go across the bridge.
You'll pass . . .

B MODELS (Read, Discuss and Perform)

1 A man stops another man on the street for directions.

M1: Excuse me. I'm looking for the ITT building. Can you tell me how to get there from here?
M2: I'm new in town myself. I don't know. Sorry.
M1: O.K. Thanks anyway.

(He stops and asks a woman passer-by)

M1: Excuse me. I'm trying to get to the ITT building. Do you know where it is?
W: Let me think . . . yes. Do you see that tall black building there?
M1: Yes, I do.
W: It's on the other side of that building. Go straight down the street here four more blocks to Mercy Street. Turn left on Mercy and go up a block. This is 3rd Avenue. The ITT building is on the corner of 4th and Mercy.
M1: Thank you. I think I'll be able to find it now.
W: You're quite welcome.

2 *A man asks a policewoman for directions.*

   M: Pardon me. Is this the way to the City Art Museum?
   P: No, I'm sorry, it isn't. The Art Museum is four blocks back in the direction you're coming from.
   M: Oh. I must have made a mistake at the last corner. Four blocks, you said?
   P: That's right. It's a large white building on this side of the street.
   M: O.K. Thank you. I'm sure I'll find it now.

3 *Two people in a car stop a young man on the street.*

   P1: Excuse me. Can you tell us how to find Court Street?
   YM: Oh, sure. You're almost there. Continue straight for another two blocks until you come to the next stop-light. That will be Court Street.
   P2: Thank you very much.
   YM: That's quite all right.

4 *A car driver asks a gas-station attendant for directions.*

   D: Excuse me. Can you tell me where the Community College is?
   A: Sure. Go up Malta Road here until you come to 156th Street. Make a left on 156th and go about a mile and a half to Southern Avenue. Turn left on Southern and go two and a half blocks. The Community College should be on your right. You can't miss it.
   D: Thank you.

C SUGGESTED ACTIVITIES (Discuss and Perform)

How would you handle the following situations?

1 You're in an English class, and a fellow student is telling you about a good restaurant he recently went to. You want to find out how to get there.
2 A new student in class asks you how to get to the nearest bus stop.
3 You invite a fellow student to your home for dinner. He/she doesn't know how to get there, so you draw a map and explain the way.

B – 3 Business Appointments / Reception Desk

A EXAMPLES

Making an Appointment

I'd like to make an appointment to see Mr. Bentley.
I'd like to make arrangements to meet with Ms. Linton.
That's fine.
That's not a good time for me.
I'm sorry, but I have other business at that time.
Would it be possible to schedule a different time?

Secretary

What is your name please?
What's the name, please?
What would you like to see Mr. Finn *about?*
What is it that you'd to meet with Ms. Katanan *about?*
How about Friday morning at 9:15?
Would Tuesday afternoon at 2:00 be convient for you?
Would Monday morning at 11:00 fit into your schedule?
What is your telephone number?
What's the number you can be reached at during the day?
Can you give me a telephone number where we can get in touch with you if there's a change in plans?

At the Reception Desk

I have an appointment with Mrs. Stanley.
I'm here to see Mr. Taylor.
My name is Phil Donnelly.
The name is Walker. Bruce Walker.

Receptionist

Let me check Mr. Leet's office.
Could you please wait a moment.
Would you mind waiting a moment?
Could you have a seat please?
Would you mind having a seat?
I'll tell Mrs. Jaine *you're here.*
Mr. Foster *will be right out.*
Ms. Lee *is ready to see you now.*
Mr. Mercer *will see you now.*
Do you have an appointment?
Is Mr. Foster *expecting you?*

B MODELS

1 A student is talking with her advisor's secretary.

    AS: Good morning. Can I help you?
    S: Yes. I'd like to make an appointment to see Dr. Fince.
    AS: Is Dr. Fince your regular advisor?
    S: Yes, but I haven't been in to see her for quite a while.
    AS: O.K. What's your name, please?

S:	Marcy Stevens.
AS:	What would you like to see Dr. Fince about?
S:	I'm going to graduate next term, so I need to see her about that.
AS:	O.K. Would Friday morning at 10:15 be convenient for you?
S:	That's fine. Thank you.
AS:	You're welcome.

2 *A businessman is making an appointment with a secretary.*

S:	Good morning. Cotter Industries. This is Robert Johnson, Western Region Sales Manager's office.
BM:	Good morning. My name is Les. Easton, from Layton Business Machines. I'd like to speak with Mr. Johnson, if I may.
S:	I'm sorry, but Mr. Johnson's not in today. I'm Mr. Johnson's secretary, Eva Jones. Can I help you?
BM:	Yes. I'd like to make arrangements to get together with Mr. Johnson sometime tomorrow or the day after. We met at a recent conference, and he asked me to stop by the office when I came to town. I'm leaving Friday evening, so it would need to be tomorrow or Friday sometime.
S:	O.K. Mr. Easton. Mr. Johnson has some time tomorrow afternoon, about 3:30. Would that fit into your schedule?
BM:	Tomorrow at 3:30 is fine.
S:	Can you give me a telephone number where we can reach you if it's necessary to?
BM:	I'm staying at the Winston Towers Hotel. Room 3414.
S:	O.K. We'll be expecting you tomorrow afternoon, then.
BM:	Thank you. Goodbye.
S:	Goodbye.

3 *A salesperson arrives for an appointment. He speaks to a receptionist.*

R:	Yes. May I help you?
SP:	Yes. I have an appointment with Ms. Thomas, the Plant Manager for 10:00. The name is Jack Morris, from Brant Associates.
R:	Yes. Let me check Ms. Thomas's office. Could you please wait a moment.

(The receptionist telephones the office)

R:	Excuse me . . . Mr. Morris. Ms. Thomas will see you now. Here, let me give you a building pass. Ms. Thomas's office is Room 2118. You can use that elevator. Turn left when you leave the elevator and go down the hall about fifteen doors.
SP:	Thank you.

(The salesperson goes to the office and speaks to a secretary)

S:	That's right.
S:	I'll tell Ms. Thomas you're here. She'll be right out. She's on the phone just now. Would you mind having a seat, please.
SP:	Yes. Of course.

(The manager comes out of her office)

M:	Good morning, Jack. Glad to meet you again.
SP:	I'm happy to see you again, too.
M:	Call me Jill. Why don't you come into my office . . . .

C SUGGESTED ACTIVITIES

Think about how you might handle the following situations.

1 You're a student, and you'd like to make an appointment with the Dean of Students. You want to major in Religion, but the school you attend has no Religion major. You call the office.
2 You live in a small town, and you have an idea about how to improve the town's bus services. You want to make an appointment with the town's mayor.
3 A radio station's advertising manager arrives for an appointment with a large department store's vice-president for advertising.

B – 4 Shopping

A EXAMPLES (Read, Discuss and Practice)

Sales Clerk
May I help you?
Can I help you with something?
Can I be of assistance?
Are you looking for something?
Is there something in particular you're looking for?
We're having a sale on . . .
This sausage is on sale today.
The baby food is on Aisle 7.
The shoe department is on the second floor.
The men's ware section is in that part of the store.
That will be $13.14.
That comes to $57.50.
Will that be cash or charge?
Do you want to pay by cash or charge?
Do you have any identification?
We need two pieces of identification.
I'm sorry, we don't take checks.

Customer
Yes. I'm looking for . . .
Can you tell me where . . .?
Yes. I'm interested in . . .
I'm just looking.
I'm being helped, thank you.
Excuse me. Can you help me?
Excuse me. I need some help.
I'd like to see that . . .
May I see that . . .
Can you show me that . . .
Is this on sale?
Is this a sale item?
When does the sale end?
I'd like to try on this coat.
Where can I try this on?
Do you have this in a larger size?
Do you have this sweater in a lighter brown?
Do you carry this in a different model?
How much is this?
What is the price of this record?
Cash.
I want to pay with a check.
I'd like to charge it.
I want to return this . . .
I'd like to exchange this . . .

B MODELS (Read, Discuss and Perform)

1 A man enters the men's clothing department of a department store. He is helped by a salesman.

   S: May I help you, Sir?
   M: No. Not at the moment. I'm just looking.
   S: That's fine, Sir. Please let me known if you need any help.
   M: Thank you. I will.

   (A few minutes later)

   M: Excuse me. Can you help me now?
   S: Of course. What is it I can do for you?
   M: I'd like to get a shirt like this, but I can't find one in my size.
   S: O.K. What size do you wear?

M: I wear a 16 ½ inch collar and 35 inch sleeve.
S: Here, let me look . . . . No, we don't have that size here. Let me check in the back. I'll be right back, Sir.

(The salesman returns)

S: I'm sorry, Sir. I couldn't find one in your size there either.
M: That's O.K. I've found a different one. Where can I try it on?
S: The dressing-room is over there, on the other side of the cash register. Please feel free to try it on.
M: Thank you.

(The customer returns after trying it on)

M: Well, it fits well. I think I'll take it.
S: Fine. I'll help you at the cash register when you're ready.

(The customer looks around a little more and goes to the register)

S: Will this be all for today, Sir?
M: I think so.
S: O.K. That's $23.50. With tax, it comes to $24.75. Will that be cash or charge?
M: I'd like to pay by check.
S: O.K. Do you have any identification? A driver's license? And a credit card?
M: Yes. Here you are.
S: Thank you very much, Sir. Come again.
M: Thank you.

2 *A man is looking for something in a drug store. He is helped by an assistant.*

M: Excuse me. Can you tell me where the after-shave lotion is?
A: Yes. It's over there on Aisle 15 – A.
M: Thank you.

3 *A woman who is shopping in a supermarket speaks with a sales clerk.*

W: Excuse me, young man. Do you have any more of this tomato sauce which is on sale?
SC: It should be over there on Aisle 10, with the other tomato sauce.
W: There's no more there.
SC: Hmmm. Maybe we're out of it already. Let me check in the back. Just a minute please.

(The shop clerk returns)

SC: I'm sorry, Ma'am. We're out of stock on that.
W: Can I have a raincheck, then, please?
SC: O.K. Just ask at the cash register.

(At the check-out stand)

SC: Will that be everything for you today?
W: Yes. I also have these coupons I'd like to redeem.
SC: O.K. *(She finishes)* O.K. That comes to $38.62.
W: O.K. Here you are.

SC: And here's your change. Here's the $1.86 back on the coupons. Thank you for shopping MKB. Have a nice day.
W: Thank you. You too.

4 A young girl who wants to return a record she bought is helped by a shop clerk.

SC: Yes, Miss. Can I help you?
YG: Yes. I want to return this record I bought the other day. It's warped, and it doesn't play well on my stereo.
SC: I see. Do you have your sales receipt?
YG: Yes. Here it is.
SC: Do you want to exchange it for another or return it for a refund?
YG: I want to return it for a refund.
SC: O.K. If you had wanted to exchange it, I could take care of it here. In order to return it, you have to take it to the courtesy desk over there by the main entrance.
YG: O.K. Thanks.

(She goes to the courtesy desk and talks with the manager)

M: Can I help you?
YG: Yes. I want to return this record I bought. It's warped and doesn't play well. Here's my sales receipt.
M: O.K. Let me see. . . . Yes, it is a little warped, isn't it. Are you sure you don't want to exchange it?
YG: Yes. I'm sure.
M: O.K. Here. It was $9.95 plus tax . . . . It came to $10.53. Here you are. Sorry to have troubled you.
YG: That's O.K. Thank you.
M: Thank you.

C SUGGESTED ACTIVITIES (Discuss and Perform)

What would you probably do in the following situations?

1 You're in a department store and want to buy a gift for a friend's birthday. You're thinking about buying her a blouse. A sales clerk comes up to you.
2 You're in a grocery store looking for cake mix. You can't find it. You ask a check-out clerk at the check-out stand.
3 You recently bought a toaster, but when you got it home, you found it didn't work very well. You want to exchange it at the store where you bought it.

B – 5 Restaurants

At a Quick-Food Restaurant

A EXAMPLES (Read, Discuss and Practice)

Next, please.
Can I help you?
What would you like to order?
Is that for here or to go?
Is that to go?
Anything to drink?
Will there be anything else?
That'll be . . .
That comes to . . .
Could you please wait a moment for your order.
Here's your order. Have a nice meal.

I'd like the . . .
I want a . . .
Let me have . . .
For here.
To go.

B MODELS (Read, Discuss and Perform)

1 A woman places an order at a quick-food restaurant. She is served by an assistant.

A: Next, please. Can I help you?
W: Yes. I'd like a de luxe hamburger and a large order of fries.
A: Is that for here or to go?
W: For here.
A: Anything to drink?
W: Yes. A grape soda.
A: O.K. That's a de luxe burger, a large fries and a grape soda. That'll be $3.86 with tax.
W: O.K. Here.
A: Four dollars . . . . That's fourteen cents change. Here you are. Can you please wait a minute for your order?
W: Sure.
A: *(A minute later)* Here's your order. Have a nice meal.
W: Thanks.

A Regular Restaurant

A EXAMPLES (Read, Discuss and Practice)

Do you have a reservation?
Could you wait a moment to be seated?
How many people?

We have reservations for a party of six.
The name is Jones.
I have 6:00 reservations for two people.

How many people in your party?
Please follow me.
Please come with me.
Here's the menu.
Your menus.
Can I take your order?
May I have your order?
What would you like to order?
Here you are, Sir.
Here's the veal *you ordered.*
Who ordered the lamb stew?
Was yours the shish kebab?
Enjoy your meal.
Is everything all right here?
Is everything O.K.?
How's your meal?
Will there be anything else?
Would you like anything else?
I'm sorry. We're out of veal.
I'm sorry. We don't have lamb.
Here's your check.
You can pay me.
I'll take care of the check for you.
Please pay as you leave.

My name is Smith.
Excuse me!
Waiter!
Waitress!
Miss!
Can I have a menu, please.
May I see a menu?
I'd like to order the chef's salad.
I'll have the chicken fricassee.
What I want is the fried chicken.
Excuse me, waiter. This fork *is a little dirty.*
Miss, this soup *is cold. Can I have it warmed up?*
I'd like to have the check, please.
May I have the check?
Check, please.
Do I pay you or as I leave?
Do I pay you or at the register?

B MODELS (Read, Discuss and Perform)

1 A man is calling a restaurant for reservations. He speaks to the receptionist.

R: Good afternoon. Ivan's Russian Restaurant.
M: Hello. I'd like to make reservations for dinner tonight.
R: Yes, Sir. How many people in your party?
M: Five. We'd like a table near a window, too, please.
R: I'll certainly see if that can be arranged. What time do you want your reservation for?
M: We'll be coming at 7:30.
R: And what is the name, please?
M: The name is Miller.
R: Thank you, Sir. We'll be expecting you at 7:30.
M: Thank you. Goodbye.
R: Goodbye.

2 A man and woman are met by the hostess while entering a restaurant.

H: Good afternoon. How many people?
W: Two.
H: O.K. Could you wait a moment to be seated?
M: Sure.

(A couple of minutes later)

H: Sorry to have kept you waiting. I'll show you to your table.
M: Thank you.
H: *(At the table)* Here you are. Your waitress will be with you in a minute. Here are your menus.

(The waitress comes)

Wa: Good afternoon. My name's Phyllis. I'll be your waitress. Would you care for a cocktail?
W: No, thank you.
Wa: O.K. Are you ready to order, then?
M: We're still thinking about it. Can we have a couple more minutes?
Wa: Of course. Take your time. I'll be back in a few minutes.

(The waitress returns)

Wa: Are you ready to order now?
M: Yes, I think so. I'll have the veal terpentini.
Wa: Yes, Sir. Would you like potatoes or rice with that, Sir?
M: Rice.
Wa: And what kind of vegetable?
M: The green peas.
Wa: O.K. And you, Ma'am?
W: I'll have the chef's salad, with blue cheese dressing.
Wa: Yes. Would either of you like something to drink?
M: Just water for me, please.
W: I'll have a diet Pepsi.
Wa: I'm sorry, we don't have diet Pepsi. Is Tab O.K.?
W: That'll be fine.
Wa: O.K. Thank you. I'll bring your orders in a few minutes.

(The waitress brings the food)

Wa: Here you are. You ordered the veal terpentini, didn't you?
M: That's right.
Wa: And the chef salad's for you?
W: Thank you.
Wa: Enjoy your meal. I'll come back in a few minutes.

(The man calls the waitress)

M: Excuse me! Waitress!

Wa: Just a minute, Sir. *(Going to them)* Yes?
M: Can I have another glass of water, please?
Wa: Yes, Sir. I'll bring it in a couple of minutes.

(The waitress brings the water)

Wa: Here's your water, Sir. Will there be anything else?
M: Yes. I'd like to have dessert. Can I see the menu again?
Wa: Yes, Sir. Here you are.

M: I'd like to have a piece of apple pie. And a cup of coffee.
Wa: Anything for you, Ma'am?
W: Nothing for me, thank you.

(After the couple finish the meal)

Wa: How was your meal? Will there be anything else?
W: Everything was quite good. I think that'll be all. May we have the check, please?
Wa: Yes. I'll bring it in a minute.

(The waitress brings the check)

Wa: Here's your check.
W: Do we pay you?
Wa: I'll take care of it for you, Ma'am.
W: Here you are.
Wa: That's thirty dollars. I'll bring your change shortly.

(The waitress returns with the change)

Wa: Here's your change. I hope you had a pleasant meal.
M: We did, thank you.
Wa: Thank you. Have a nice evening.
M: You, too.

(The woman leaves the tip on the table as they leave)

C SUGGESTED ACTIVITIES

What would you probably do in the following situations?

1 You go to a quick-food restaurant in a city where you are visiting. You order your lunch.
2 You're going to go out for dinner with a few friends. You have to make the reservations.
3 You enter a restaurant, but you don't have reservations.
4 A business person is having dinner with an acquaintance. They are met by the hostess, who seats them at the table. They want to have a relaxed meal.

B – 6 Doctor / Dentist / Hospital / Pharmacy

A EXAMPLES (Read, Discuss and Practice)

Are you a patient of Dr. Lee?
Do you have an appointment?
Please be seated. The doctor will be with you soon.
Dr. Frank *will see you in a minute.*
The doctor will see you now.
What seems to be the trouble?
What's the problem?
Do you have any other symptoms?
What other symptoms do you have?
O.K. Let's take a look.
You're going to need some tests.
I'd like to have you take some tests . . . .
Do you have health insurance?
May I see your health insurance card?

I'd like to make an appointment to see Dr. Alberts.
I have a 2:00 appointment with Dr. Stevens.
I'm here to see Dr. Stevens.
I'm here to see Dr. Rezza.
I've been having stomach pains.
I have a toothache.
I'd like to have this prescription filled.
Can I have this prescription filled?

B MODELS (Read, Discuss and Perform)

1 A woman is calling to make a doctor's appointment. She speaks to his receptionist.

R: Good morning. Dr. Harmon's office.
W: Hello. I'd like to make an appointment to see Dr. Harmon.
R: What is the name, please?
W: My name is Nelson. Beverly Nelson.
R: Are you a patient of Dr. Harmon's?
W: No, I'm not. But I would like to become a patient.
R: I'm sorry, but Dr. Harmon is not taking any more patients.
W: Martha Weber, a friend of mine who is a long-time patient of Dr. Harmon, suggested that I should call.
R: Hmmm. O.K. I guess I can try to squeeze one more appointment in. What's the trouble?
W: I've been having severe recurrent headaches for the past month now. I've also been having dizzy spells and nausea.
R: O.K. How would Thursday at 3:00 be?
W: That sounds fine, thank you.
R: Now, what is your address and telephone number?
W: My address is . . . .

2 *A man is at a dental office's reception desk. He speaks to the receptionist.*

- **R:** Good afternoon. Can I help you?
- **M:** Yes. I have an appointment to see Dr. Lowrey.
- **R:** What's the name, please?
- **M:** Tyler. Willy Tyler. The appointment is for 10.30.
- **R:** Yes, here it is. Could you please be seated. The doctor will be able to see you in a few minutes.

(Twenty minutes later)

- **R:** Mr. Tyler. You can go in now. This way, please.
- **M:** Thank you.

(He enters the treatment room and is greeted by the doctor)

- **Dr:** Good morning, Mr. Tyler. What seems to be the problem?
- **M:** I have a really bad toothache. And a filling fell out.
- **Dr:** Hmmm. O.K. Why don't you sit here and I'll have a look at it.

3 *A woman enters a hospital emergency room carrying her son. She speaks to a receptionist.*

- **R:** Can I help you?
- **W:** Yes. My son fell down a flight of stairs at home. It seems like he may have broken his arm.
- **R:** O.K. What's the name, please?
- **W:** Tracy. Mary Tracy. My son's name is Michael.
- **R:** O.K. Has he or anyone in your family been treated here before?
- **W:** No. This is the first time.
- **R:** Do you have health insurance?
- **W:** Yes. I have Blue Cross. Here's my card.

R: O.K. Right this way. The doctor will be in to see your son in just a minute. Please wait in this room.
W: O.K. Thank you. *(To son)* It's going to be all right, Mikey.

4 A woman enters her doctor's examination room.

Dr: Good morning, Mrs. Jones. What seems to be the problem?
W: Hello, Dr. Hinton. I've been having pretty bad stomach pains for a couple of weeks now. Nothing I've been taking seems to help.
Dr: I see. Where are these pains?
W: Right here. *(He touches her there)* Ouch! Right there.
Dr: How frequently do you have them and how long do they last?
W: About three of four times a week, for three to four hours.
Dr: O.K. Would you mind lying down here on the examining table. I'd like to have a better look . . . .

(After the examination)

Dr: Well, Mrs. Jones. I'd like to have you take some tests.
W: Is it something serous? What kind of tests?
Dr: It might not be serious. The tests are routine ones.
W: What do you think it is?
Dr: It could be a number of things. There's nothing I can really say without the tests. Why don't you get up now, and the nurse will give you the slips to take to the lab. and schedule another appointment.
W: O.K. Thank you, doctor.
Dr: That's O.K. We'll be seeing you again soon.

(With the nurse at the reception desk)

N: O.K. Mrs. Jones. Here are the slips you'll need for the lab. tests. The lab. is just down the hall, Room 446. Would you be able to come in again the end of the week, say, Friday at 2:00 in the afternoon?
W: Yes. I can come.
N: O.K., then. Please have the tests done now, and we'll be expecting you on Friday.
W: Thank you.

5 A man brings a prescription to a pharmacist to be filled.

P: Can I help you, Sir?
M: Yes. I'd like to have this prescription filled, please.
P: O.K. It'll take a few minutes. I'll call your name when it's ready.
M: O.K. I have some time.

(The pharmacist calls the man's name)

P: Mr. Learner?
M: Yes.
P: Here you are. That's two tablets four times a day.
M: O.K. Do I take them before or after meals?
P: Either is O.K. Take them with plenty of water, though. Any questions?
M: No. I don't think so.
P: O.K. That will be $15.50.

C SUGGESTED ACTIVITIES (Discuss and Perform)

What would you do if you were in the following situations?

1 You're new in town, and you want to make a dentist's appointment.
2 You haven't been feeling well lately, and you've made a doctor's appointment. You're waiting in the examining room when the doctor comes in.
3 You need to have a prescription filled, and you take it to a local drug store.

B – 7 Services: Barber/Beauty Shop/Cleaners

A EXAMPLES (Read, Discuss and Practice)

How would you like it cut?
What do you want me to do?
What would you like done with it?
Now sit back and relax.
How does this look?
Does this look O.K.?
How's this?
Is there anything else you'd like to have done?
We'll have them ready on Friday.
Here are your tickets.
Don't forget your tickets when you come to pick up your things.
Please bring your tickets.

I'd like to have a little trimmed on the sides and back.
I just want the back and sides shortened a little.
Just take a little off the top.
That looks fine.
Could you trim a little more.
I'd like to have this suit cleaned and pressed.
I want to have these pants dry-cleaned.
I'd like to pick up my cleaning.

B MODELS (Read, Discuss and Perform)

1 *A man is sitting in the waiting area of a barber's shop.*

B: I think you're next, aren't you, Sir?
M: Yes. That's right.
B: Here, have a seat. Make yourself comfortable. How would you like it cut?
M: I'd like to have the sides and back trimmed a little, and take about an inch off the top.
B: O.K. Now, just sit back and relax.

(After the haircut is finished)

B: O.K., Sir. How's this?
M: That looks just fine.
B: Good. That will be $7.00.
M: O.K. Here's $7.00, and here's something for you.
B: Thank you very much, Sir. Have a nice day.

2 *A woman is calling a beauty shop beautician for an appointment.*

B: Hello. Nancy's House of Hair Style.
W: Hello. I'd like to make an appointment to have my hair done.
B: Is there anyone in particular you'd like to have work on you?
W: Yes. I'd like to have an appointment with Liz.
B: O.K. What would you like to have done?
W: I'd just like to have a cut and wash.
B: That's fine. Is there any particular day?
W: Uhmm . . . . Yes . . . . How would Friday be?
B: Yes. Liz is here on Fridays. How about 2:00.

W: That would be fine.
B: And what's the name, please?
W: Stevenson. Betty Stevenson.
B: O.K., Betty. We'll be expecting you at 2:00 on Friday.
W: Thank you.

3 *A woman arrives at a beauty shop for her appointment.*

B: May I help you?
W: Yes. I have a 2:00 appointment with Liz. The name is Stevenson.
B: Yes. Here's your name. She's with someone right now, but she should be finished in a few minutes. Would you mind waiting?
W: No, not at all.

(A few minutes later)

B: Miss Stevenson, Liz is ready to see you now. She'll take care of you at chair 15.
W: Thank you.

(The hairdresser comes and begins talking)

H: Well, how are you today, Miss Stevenson?
W: I'm fine, thank you. And you?
H: Quite well, thank you. Now, what would you like to have done?
W: I'd like to have it cut short, with a flip on the back and sides.
H: Uhmmm . . . sort of like this?
W: Yes, that's it.
H: O.K. Now, sit back and relax. This will take a little time.

(After the cut, wash and dry)

H: How does this look, Miss Stevenson?
W: That looks just fine to me.
H: Is there anything else you'd like to have done today?
W: No, not today. How much is that?
H: That'll be $15.00.
W: O.K. Here you are. And this is for you.
H: Why, thank you, Miss Stevenson. Have a nice day.
W: You too.

4 *A man brings some clothes to a dry-cleaner.*

C: Can I help you, Sir?
M: Yes. I'd like to have these pants cleaned and pressed. I'd also like to have this sports coat cleaned.
C: O.K. We can have them ready for you the day after tomorrow.
M: Fine.
C: What is the name, please?
M: Hamilton.
C: And your address and phone number?
M: 144 South Street Apartment 3. Telephone number 345-6789.
C: O.K., Sir. Here are your tickets. Don't forget to bring them with you when you come to pick everything up.
M: O.K. I will.

5 *A man returns to pick up his cleaning at a dry-cleaners.*

    C: Can I help you, Sir?
    M: Yes. I'd like to pick up these things. *(He gives the tickets)*
    C: O.K. Just a minute, Sir.

(The cleaner returns with the cleaning)

    C: Here you are. That will be $12.50.
    M: O.K. Here you are.
    C: That's $13.00 And here's your change. Please come again.
    M: I'm sure I'll have to.

C SUGGESTED ACTIVITIES (Discuss and Perform)

How might you handle the following situations?

1 You need to have a haircut, and a friend recommends a good place to go. You want to give it a try.
2 A woman arrives at a beauty parlor for her appointment. She wants to get a permanent.
3 You need to have some clothes cleaned at a dry-cleaners.

B – 8 Cars: Gas / Service

A EXAMPLES (Read, Discuss and Practice)

I'd like $8.00 of the unleaded.
Let me have $10.00 of the premium.
Fill 'er up with the regular.
Please check under the hood, too.
Could you check the oil and water.
I'd like to have my car looked at.
I'm having some trouble with my car and need to have it repaired.
I need to have some work done on my car.
When can you have it done by?
When will it be finished by?
When's it going to be ready?

Can I help you?
Want me to check under the hood?
Check the oil and water?
Everything's O.K.
You need a quart of oil.
Your oil's down about a quart.
What's the problem?
What kind of trouble are you having with it.
Come back at 4:00.
We should have it done by 5:00.
It should be ready by noon.

B MODELS (Read, Discuss and Perform)

1 A man stops at a self-service gas station requiring pre-payment and speaks to an attendant.

  M: Hi. I'd like to have $12.00 of the unleaded premium.
  A: O.K. Go ahead.

  (He fills the tank and drives off)

2 *A woman stops at a full-service gas station.*

A: Can I help you, Ma'am?
W: Yes. Could you fill it up with the unleaded, please?
A: O.K. Want me to check under the hood, too?
W: Would you please?
A: Sure thing.

(The attendant brings and shows the oil dip-stick)

A: O.K., Ma'am. You're down about a quart. Want me to add some?
W: Would you please?

(The attendant finishes)

A: O.K. With the oil, it comes to $21.50.
W: Here you are.
A: And here's your change. Have a nice day. Drive safely.

3 *A man calls an automobile repair shop about his car and speaks to a mechanic.*

CM: Hello. Joe's Repair Shop.
M: Hello. I'm having some problems with my car, and I'd like to have it looked at.
CM: O.K. What kind of car is it?
M: A 1980 Pinto.
CM: And what's the problem?
M: It keeps stalling.
CM: O.K. Why don't you bring it by tomorrow morning anytime after 8:00, and we'll have a look at it. What's the name?
M: Fenster.

(The man takes the car to the shop at 8:30 the next morning)

CM: Can I help you?
M: I'm bringing in my car to have it worked on. A 1980 Pinto. My name's Fenster.
CM: O.K. I'll have a look at it this morning. Come back at 12:00.
M: 12:00. O.K. Thanks.

(The man returns to the shop at 12:00.)

M: Hi. Is my car ready yet?
CM: Yeah. It was nothing serious. Just a sticking carburetor.
M: Well, that's good news.
CM: Yeah. Here's the bill. It comes to $16.50.
M: O.K. Will you take a check?
CM: Sure. *(Taking the check)* This your current address and phone?
M: Yeah.

C SUGGESTED ACTIVITIES (Discuss and Perform)

How might you handle the following situations?

1 You stop at a self-service gas station for gas. A sign on the pump says pre-payment only.
2 You're driving on the freeway, and the oil light on your car comes on. You slowly drive to the next exit and drive up to a service station.
3 You go to your car in the morning and find a flat tire. You change tires, and bring the flat to a station to have it fixed.

B – 9 Beggars / Salespeople / Solicitors / Proselytizers

A EXAMPLES (Read, Discuss and Practice)

Can you let me have a quarter?
Excuse me, Mister. Can you spare me a quarter?
I have here . . .
I'm selling . . .
We're offering . . .
Would you like to contribute to . . .
Would you care to help support . . .
We're collecting for . . .
Could you give something to . . .
Would you be interested in . . .
Would you care to join . . .

Here you go.
No.
I said no.
I'm not interested.
I don't need any.
I have no need for costmetics.
I said I'm not interested.
Stop bothering me.
If you don't stop bothering me I'm going to call the police.

B MODELS (Read, Discuss and Perform)

1 A young boy stops a man on the street.

YB: Excuse me, Sir. Can you let me have a quarter?
M: Huh? Uhm . . . what for?
YB: I need to call home, and I don't have any money.
M: O.K. Here you go.
YB: Thanks, Mister.

2 A beggar approaches a man walking along the street.

B: Hey, Mister, can you spare me a quarter?
M: No.
B: C'mon, man. Have a heart. I ain't eaten in days.
M: I said no. *(He walks away)*

3 A woman receives a telephone call at her home from a salesperson.

W: Hello.
S: Hello. Is this Ms. Jamie Watson?
W: Yes.
S: I'm calling from the *Plainsville Times,* Ms. Watson. Do you currently have a subscription to the *Times?*
W: No, I don't. But I'm not interested in one.
S: What I'm calling about is a special introductory subscription to the *Times.* We give you two free weeks of delivery . . . .
W: Excuse me, but, as I said, I'm not interested.

S: After your two free weeks, you have no obligation to continue if you choose not to . . . .
W: That's O.K. I'm not interested. And don't call me back. *(She hangs up)*

4 *A woman is stopped by a religious group member at the airport.*

RGM: Here you are, Ma'am, a flower for you. Love and peace to you. Would you like to contribute to the Spiritual Reunion Church? Your money will be used to help build love and . . .
W: I'm not interested in contributing.
RGM: But, Ma'am! A small gift would mean so much to so many people . . . .
W: I said I'm not interested, and don't bother me. *(She walks away)*

5 *A woman answers her doorbell and a proselytizer woman is standing there.*

W: Yes? What is it?
P: Hi. My name's Jan. I'd like to talk with you about something that may be very important for you.
W: What is it?
P: I'm from the New Word Bible Association, and I was wondering if you'd be interested in joining our study group.
W: No, I don't think so.
P: We meet once a week, for fellowship and bible reading. Do you have a bible, Ma'am?
W: Yes, I do, but I'm not interested in joining a bible study group. If I am, I'll call you. Thank you.

C SUGGESTED ACTIVITIES (Discuss and Perform)

What would you probably do in the following situations?

1 You're approached by a beggar on the street.
2 Your doorbell rings, and when you answer it, you find a salesman trying to sell home encyclopedias.
3 A religious group member asks you for a contribution on a downtown street.

B – 10 Bargaining: Flea Markets / Garage Sales / Second-Hand Shops

A EXAMPLES (Read, Discuss and Practice)

How much is this?
What are you asking for . . ?
How much do you want for . . ?
What? For that?
That's much too much.
That sounds a little high.
That's a little more than I want to pay.
I give you $25.00 for it.
I'll pay you $5.00 for it.
I'll take it if you cut the price to $75.00.
That's still too much.
I'll make one last offer: $2.00.
My last offer is $15.00.

The price is on it.
I'm asking $1,200.00.
How much are you willing to offer for it?
How much do you think it's worth?
Make an offer.
That's not enough.
I can't let it go for that.
I tell you what. I'll give it to you for $35.00.
You can have it for $500.00.
$20.00 and it's yours.
The absolute lowest I can go is $250.00.
That's as low as I'll go.

B MODELS (Read, Discuss and Perform)

1 A young husband and wife are talking with a man at a flea market.

H: Excuse me, how much are you asking for that spinning-wheel?
M: That? The price is $150.00.
W: What? For that? It's not in very good condition. I've seen better ones for a lot less.
M: Maybe, but this is a very special model. With a little work, it'll be worth a lot more than $150.00.

COMMUNICATING IN ENGLISH VOLUME 3

H: It is nice, but that's a little more than we want to pay. We'll take it if you cut the price to $100.00.
M: You must be kidding. I can't let it go for that. I tell you what: I'll take off $20.00. You can have it for $130.00.
W: Take off another $10.00 and it's a deal.
M: Hmmm . . . . Well . . . . O.K. $125.00. That's the lowest I'll go.
H: It's a deal. Here you are: 50 . . . 100 . . . 120 . . . $125.00.
M: O.K. Listen, take good care of it. You got a really good bargain there.
H: Yeah. We think we did too. See you again some time.
M: Yeah. Stop by again some time.

2 A woman stops by a countryside second-hand shop.

W1: Excuse me, how much are you asking for that set of glasses?
W2: Those? Those are $5.00 for the set of six.
W1: Really. Isn't that a little expensive?
W2: What would you say they're worth?
W1: I'll give you $2.50 for the set.
W2: No. They're worth more than that.
W1: O.K. $3.00.
W2: $4.00 and you can have them.
W1: $3.00.
W2: O.K. O.K. $3.00 and they're yours.
W1: O.K. Here you go. *(She hands her a $5.00 bill)*
W2: And here's your change: $2.00.
W1: Do you have a bag to put them in?
W2: I'm sorry, I don't.
W1: That's O.K. I'll just put them in here.
W2: Why don't you look around some more?
W1: Thank you. I think I will.

C SUGGESTED ACTIVITIES (Discuss and Perform)

What would you probably do if you were in the following situations?

1 You go to a garage sale and see an antique plate. You know that the plate is worth much more than the price on it.
2 You want to buy a used coffee table for your apartment, and you go to a second-hand furniture shop. You see one you like.
3 You read an advertisement for a second-hand car in the newspaper. You call about it and decide to go and see it. You're talking with the owner, and you feel he's asking too much for it.

C – 1 Telephone / Telegram

A EXAMPLES (Read, Discuss and Practice)

Hello.
Hello. Jenson Residence.
Hello. Foster Industries.
I'm sorry. You must have the wrong number.
I think you have the wrong number.
Who's this calling?
Who shall I say is calling?
May I ask who's calling?
Can I take a message?
Shall I have her call you back?
Would you like him to call you back?
Please hold a moment.
Can I put you on hold a minute.
Would you mind holding a minute.
Operator.
Information for what city?
What is the message, please.

Hello.
Is Jim *there*?
May I speak with Fran, *please.*
Is Mrs. Winston *in*?
Is that the Police Department?
No message.
The message is . . .
Could you have him call me at 243-8576?
I'd like to have the telephone number of . . .
I'd like to make a long-distance collect call to . . .
I want to make an international call to . . .
I want to send a telegram to . . .
The message is . . .

B MODELS (Read, Discuss and Perform)

1 A man is calling an acquaintance on the phone. His wife answers.

W: Hello.
M: Hello. Can I speak to Steve, please?
W: Yes. Just a minute. Who shall I say is calling?
M: This is Tom Alberts. I work in the same office as Steve.
W: O.K. Just a minute, please.

(The acquaintance comes to the phone)

A: Hello?
M: Hi, Steve. This is Tom. How's it going?

2 A person dials a wrong number.

P1: Hello?
P2: Hello? Maria?
P1: Oh, I'm sorry. You must have the wrong number.
P2: I'm sorry. Is this 811-9876?
P1: No, it isn't.
P2: I'm sorry to have bothered you. Thank you.
P1: That's O.K. No problem.

3 A man is making a business call. A secretary answers.

S1: Good morning. Portland Security Insurance.

105

M: Hello. May I speak to Mr. Jones in the Claims Department?
S1: Could you please hold? I'll transfer your call.
M: O.K.

(The call is transformed and a different secretary answers)

S2: Hello. Portland Security Insurance. Claims Department.
M: Hello. May I speak with Mr. Jones please.
S2: I'm sorry. Mr Jones is out of the office just now. Can I take a message or have him call you?
M: Yeah. My name is Larry Trains. I'm calling about a car accident I recently had, and I need to talk to him about it.
S2: O.K. Sir. Shall I have Mr. Jones call you?
M: Uhm . . . no. I won't be near a phone most of the day. What time do you expect him back?
S2: He should be back after 2:30 p.m.
M: O.K. I'll call back then.
S2: That would be fine. He'll be expecting your call.
M: O.K. Goodbye.
S2: Goodbye.

4 *A woman dials 555-1212 for information. The operator answers.*

O: Information for what city, please?
W: Stevensville, Ohio.
O: Go ahead, please.
W: Can you give me the number of a Jim Jones on Mercy Road?
O: Yes. That number is 899-6758.
W: 899-6758. Thank you.
O: You're quite welcome.

5 *A young woman is making a collect call from a pay phone. She speaks to the operator.*

O: Operator. Can I help you?
YW: Yes. I'd like to make a long distance person-to-person collect call to a Mr Frank Fruman in Billings, Wyoming. The number is 566-978-7465.
O: O.K. What number are you calling from, Miss?
YW: The number here is 234-5412.
O: And what is your name, please?
YW: The name is Gregoria Hillman.
O: Thank you. Please hold a minute.

(The phone rings and is answered)

O: Hello. I have a collect person-to-person call for a Mr Frank Fruman. Is he there?
M: Yes.
O: I have a collect person-to-person call from a Gregoria Hillman. Will you accept the charges?
M: Yes, I will.
O: O.K. Go ahead, please.
YW: Thank you. Frank. How are you?
M: Greg. This is really a surprise . . . .

6 *A man wants to make an international phone call. He is helped by the operator.*

O1: Operator.
M: Yes. I'd like to place an international call to Japan.
O1: Yes, Sir. Can you hold a minute, please, and I'll transfer your call to the international operator.

(The operator transfers the call)

O2: International operator.
M: I'd like to make an international call to Japan.
O2: What is the number please?
M: The number is 0465-43-9857.
O2: 0465-43-9857. Yes, Sir. Please hold on. *(The phone rings)* I'm sorry, Sir, but no one answers. Can you try placing your call again later.
M: Yeah. O.K. Thanks.
O2: Thank you, Sir.

7 *A woman wants to send a telegram. She speaks to a clerk at the Telegraph Office.*

C: Hello. Western Union.
W: Hello. I'd like to send a telegram to Atlanta, Georgia.
C: O.K. What is your name, please?
W: My name is Leslie Starr.
C: And what is your telephone number?
W: 489-9189.
C: And your address?
W: 1410, 53rd Street, Apartment 622, Portland, Oregon, 98765.
C: And who is the message to?
W: Bill and Ginny Martin. 243, 15th Street, Atlanta, Georgia.
C: And what is the message, please?
W: The message is: DEAR MOM AND DAD, HAPPY 25TH. HOPE YOU HAVE MANY MORE. LOVE. LESLIE AND MIKE.
C: O.K. That's Dear Mom and Dad stop happy 25th stop hope you have many more stop love stop Leslie and Mike stop.
W: That's right. How much will that be?
C: That'll be . . . just a minute . . . $2.50.
W: O.K. When will it get there?
C: It'll be phoned in as soon as it arrives, and a copy should arrive the next day in the mail.
W: Fine, Thank you.
C: Would you like to have a copy of the message sent to you?
W: No. That's not necessary.
C: O.K. Thank you for calling Western Union.

C SUGGESTED ACTIVITIES

How would you manage the following situations?

1 You're calling a friend, but you dial a wrong number the first time.
2 You want to make a collect call to a friend in another part of the country.
3 You want to call your parents, who live in another country.
4 You want to send a telegram to a friend who is getting married.

COMMUNICATING IN ENGLISH VOLUME 3

C – 2 Emergencies: Medical / Fire / Police

A EXAMPLES (Read, Discuss and Practice)

Emergency.
What is the location?
Where is the accident?
Where are you calling from?
What's the problem?
Is anyone hurt?
Is there a fire?
How long ago did it happen?
Please hold on.

I need an ambulance.
I need a medical unit.
I want to report a fire.
I want to report an accident.
I want to report a burglary in progress.
I want to report an attack in progress.
I want a policeman

B MODELS (Read, Discuss and Perform)

1 *A man calls the emergency telephone operator's number for an ambulance.*

    EO: Emergency.
    M: Yes. We need an ambulance.
    EO: What is the location?
    M: I'm calling from 645 Melrose Street. Apartment 311.
    EO: And what is the problem?
    M: We have a man who seems to be having a heart attack. He has also fallen and hit his head.
    EO: O.K. Hang on. We'll have an emergency vehicle there as soon as possible.

2 *A woman calls the operator about a fire.*

    O: Operator.
    W: Operator. I want to report a fire.

O: O.K. Can you please hold? I'll connect you with the Fire Department.
W: I'll hold.
(The operator transfers the call to the Fire Department)
FD: Fire Department.
W: I want to report a fire.
FD: Where is the fire?
W: It's in an apartment building on Phillips Street.
FD: What's the street number?
W: It's on the 1100 block, between John and Foster Streets.
FD: Is anyone hurt?
W: I don't known.
FD: How many stories is the apartment building?
W: About eight or ten stories.
FD: What floor is the fire on?
W: On the top floors.
FD: O.K. Please hang on. We'll send out fire equipment. . .

3 *A woman calls the emergency telephone operator's number.*

EO: Emergency.
W: Hello. I want to report a house break-in in progress.
EO: Yes, Ma'am. What is the address, please?
W: 544 Quincy Avenue. A man is trying to break in a side window.
EO: O.K., Ma'am. We'll have a patrol car there soon. Hang on.

4 *A man calls the emergency telephone operator's number.*

EO: Emergency.
M: Yes. I want to report an accident.
EO: Where is the accident?
M: On the corner of Martin Street and 53rd Avenue.
EO: Is anyone hurt?
M: Yes. A man and woman seem to be pretty badly hurt.
EO: Is there a fire?
M: No, but there's gasoline on the street.
EO: O.K. We'll send help in a few minutes. Please hold on.

C SUGGESTED ACTIVITIES (Discuss and Perform)

If you were in the following situations, what would you do?
1 You're at home by yourself, and one of your children has just electrocuted himself.
2 You're cooking, and suddenly your stove catches on fire.
3 It's late at night, and you hear a woman's scream outside your window.

C – 3 Public Transportation: Bus and Taxi

A EXAMPLES (Read, Discuss and Practice)

Bus
Can I get a downtown bus here?
Does the number 8 bus stop here?
Is this the bus to the Waterfront?
Does this bus go to the Museum?
Where can I get the #2 bus?
What bus can I take to get to the downtown Airline Terminal?
What's the fare?
How much is the fare?
When does the next #2 bus come?
How often does it stop here?
Please tell me when we get there.
Can you let me know when we arrive?

You take the number 18 bus.
You get on on 15th Avenue.
You pick up the #50 bus at the corner of 3rd Avenue and Pine Street.
You get off at the City Hall.
You need to transfer to the #35 at the Transit Park.
The fare is 60¢.
Pay as you get on.
Pay as you get off.
It runs every hour on the hour.
There is a bus every forty minutes.
One should be along in a few minutes.

Taxi
Taxi!
I want to go to . . .
I'd like to go to . . .
Please take me to . . .
What is the fare?
How much is that?
Here you are.
Here you go.
Keep the change.
Could you please wait.

Where to?
Where do you want to go?
Where is it you want to go?
Here we are.
Here you go: the Bus Station.
That'll be $5.25
That's $3.50
The fare is $6.40.

B MODELS: Bus (Read, Discuss and Perform)

1 A man asks another man and a woman at a bus stop about a bus.

    M1: Excuse me, can I get a downtown bus here?
    M2: No. These are all uptown buses. You can get a downtown bus over on 3rd Street. That's one block in that direction.
    M1: Thanks a lot.
    M2: Don't mention it.

(He goes to 3rd Street)

    M: Excuse me. Do the downtown busses stop here?
    W: Yes. You can take either a number 17 or a number 63.
    M: Do you happen to know when the next one stops here.
    W: One should be along in a few minutes.
    M: Thank you.

2 *A woman asks a bus driver if it's the correct bus.*

    W: Excuse me, is this the bus to the City Trade Center?
    D: No. You have to take a Market Street Bus. A #8.
    W: Will one be along soon?
    D: One should be coming in about five or ten minutes.
    W: O.K. Thank you.

(She gets off and waits. The next bus comes)

    W: Excuse me. Does this bus go to the City Trade Center?
    D: Yep.
    W: How much is the fare?
    D: 75c. Pay when you get off.
    W: Can you tell me when we get there?
    D: Yeah. I'll announce it.

(The bus arrives at the City Trade Center)

    D: City Trade Center.
    W: *(Paying the fare and getting off).* Thank you.

3 *A tourist is calling the city bus information center.*

    IC: Good morning. Metro Bus System. Can I help you?
    T: Yes. What bus do I take to get from the Holiday House Hotel to the City Art Museum?
    IC: O.K. Let's see . . . You need to take two busses: the #71 and #82. You can pick up the #71 on the corner of Mercy Street and 5th Avenue, two blocks east of the hotel. You get off at Vine Street and 9th, and transfer to the #82. You take that to Vine Street and 25th. The museum is one block from the bus stop there.
    T: Uhmmm . . . O.K. How often does the #71 bus run?
    IC: It runs ever forty-five minutes starting at 8:00 in the morning. So, that's 8 a.m., 8:45 a.m., 9:30 a.m., 10:15 a.m. and so on.
    T: I see. O.K. Thank you very much for your help.
    IC: Thank you for taking Metro.

MODELS: Taxi (Read, Discuss and Perform)

1 *A woman wants a taxi and sees one coming down the street.*

    W: *(Waving her hand)*

(The taxi-driver pulls up and stops. She gets in)

    TD: Yes, Ma'am. Where to?
    W: I'd like to go to the McManus Restaurant, on 5th Avenue.

(The taxi arrives at the restaurant)

    TD: O.K. Here we are.
    W: How much is that?
    TD: That'll be $3.35.
    W: Here's $4.00. Keep the change.
    TD: Thank you.

2 *A woman is calling a taxi company for a taxi.*

    TC: Hello, Acme Taxi.
    W: Yes. I'd like to have a taxi pick me up at my apartment. The address is 468 Shen Street. It's the Franklin Arms.
    TC: O.K. 468 Shen . . . the Franklin Arms. And what's the name?
    W: Crawford.
    TC: O.K. Mrs Crawford. We'll have a taxi there in ten minutes.
    W: Thank you.

C SUGGESTED ACTIVITIES (Discuss and Perform)

What would you do in the following situations?

1 You're in a new city, and you want to get a bus downtown.
2 You're at home and want to have a taxi come and pick you up.
3 You're shopping downtown, and want to take a taxi home.

C – 4 Bank

A EXAMPLES (Read, Discuss and Practice)

Next, please.
Next person in line, please.
Can I help the next person?
This window is open.
What currency do you want to exchange?
The current exchange rate is 2.6 marks *to the dollar.*
Do you have an account at this bank?
We do not cash non-customer checks drawn on other banks.
There is a $4.00 check-cashing fee for non-customers.
Please sign the back.
Please endorse the back.

I want to change some French francs into dollars.
I'd like to cash a traveler's check.
I want to buy some traveler's checks.
I'd like to cash this check.
I want to deposit this check into my checking account.
I want to withdraw some money from my savings account.
I'd like to transfer some money from my savings account into my checking account.
I'd like to check the balance in my savings account.

B MODELS (Read, Discuss and Perform)

1 A traveler is exchanging money at a bank. He is helped by a bank clerk.

BC: Can I help you?
T: Yes. I want to change some money.
BC: What currency? And how much?
T: I want to change 200,000 Japanese yen into dollars.
BC: O.K. The current exchange rate is 215 yen to the dollar. That would come to $930.23.
T: O.K. Here is 20 . . . 40 . . . 60 . . . 80 . . . 100 . . . 20 . . . 40 . . . 60 . . . 80 . . . 200,000 yen.
BC: O.K. Let me see . . . 200,000 yen. That's $930.23, as I said before. Here you are.
T: And I'd like to have $800.00 in traveler's checks.
BC: O.K. We carry these traveler's checks. Will they do?
T: Quite well.
BC: What denominations would you like?
T: I want four $100, four $50 and ten $20 checks.
BC: O.K. Please fill out this form . . . *(The man fills it out).* That looks O.K. That will be $808.00 with the service fee.
T: O.K. $808. Here you are.
BC: That's fine. And here are your checks. Don't forget to sign them before anything can happen to them.
T: O.K. Thank you.
BC: We're glad to be of service.

2 *A woman wants to cash a traveler's check at a bank. She speaks to the bank clerk.*

    BC: Next person in line, please. Can I help you?
    W: Yes. I want to cash a traveler's check.
    BC: O.K. For how much.
    W: $100.00.
    BC: O.K. Here you are . . . 20 . . . 40 . . . 60 . . . 80 . . . $100.00.
    W: And can I have a ten and two fives for this twenty?
    BC: Of course. Here you are.
    W: And one more thing . . . can I have change of a dollar, too?
    BC: Certainly. Will three quarters, two dimes and a nickel do?
    W: Yes. Thank you.
    BC: You're welcome.

3 *A woman wants to cash a check at a bank where she has no account. A bank clerk attends to her.*

    BC: This window is open. Next please.
    W: I'd like to cash this check.
    BC: O.K. Do you have an account with this bank?
    W: No, I don't.
    BC: In that case, there's a $5.00 check-cashing fee for noncustomers.
    W: Uhmm . . . that's a lot, isn't it?
    BC: I'm sorry, but it's bank policy.
    W: Well . . . O.K. Here.
    BC: O.K. Please sign on the back, and I'll need to see some identification.
    W: Will a driver's licence do?
    BC: Yes, and a credit card if you have one.
    W: I don't have one. I do have an identity card from my school.
    BC: That will do. *(She looks at the identification)* O.K. Here you are . . . $57.20 minus the $5.00 fee is $52.20.
    W: O.K. Thank you.

4 *A man wants to deposit and transfer some money in his accounts. He speaks to the bank clerk.*

    BC: Can I help the next person in line, please.
    M: Yes. I want to deposit $400.00 of this check into my checking account and get the rest in cash. I also want to withdraw $250.00 from my savings account and transfer that to my checking account, too.
    BC: O.K. Please endorse this check on the back. Let's see . . . $400.00 of this into your checking account, and you also want to transfer $250.00 from savings to checking. O.K. That's a total of $650.00 into your checking account. And here is your $57.20 back from the check you deposited.
    M: Great. Thank you.
    BC: Don't forget your deposit and withdrawal slips. Here you are.
    M: Oh, yeah. Thanks again.

C SUGGESTED ACTIVITIES (Discuss and Perform)

How might the following situations be handled?

1 You are from another country, and you have just arrived on a tour in America. You want to change some money into dollars.
2 You're planning a trip, and you need to buy some traveler's checks. You go to a bank downtown.
3 You've just received a check from a friend, and you want to cash it at your bank.

C – 5 Post Office

A EXAMPLES (Read, Discuss and Practice)

Next, please.
Can I help the next person.
What's inside?
How do you want to send this: first-class or parcel post?
Do you want to send this by air mail or surface mail?
Do you want to insure it?
Please fill out this form.
Please fill out this customs declaration.
This package isn't wrapped properly. We can't accept it.

I'd like to have five 20¢ stamps.
I want five aerograms to Brazil.
I want to send this package to Thailand.
I'd like to send this letter by certified mail.
I want to send this package book-rate to Mexico.
I want to insure this package.
How much would this be air-mail?
I would like to buy a money order.

B MODELS (Read, Discuss and Perform)

1 A man wants to buy some stamps and aerograms. A post office clerk helps him.

C: Next person in line, please.
M: Yes. I want ten 20¢ stamps and five air mail stamps to Italy.
C: O.K. Here you are. Will that be all?
M: Yes, that's it.
C: O.K. That comes to . . . $2.00 and $1.55 . . . that's $3.55.
M: Here you are. Thank you.

2 A woman wants to send a letter and some packages. She is attended to by a clerk.

C: Good morning. Can I help you?
W: Yes. I want to send this letter to Saudi Arabia, this small package to New York, and this package to Venezuela.
C: O.K. Let's take care of the letter first. This letter is one and a half ounces, so that's 96c. Now, this package to New York. This is four pounds five ounces. How do you want to send this, first-class or parcel post?
W: How much would it be by each?
C: It would be $1.25 by parcel post and $6.75 first-class.
W: I'll send it parcel post.
C: Do you want to insure it?
W: No, I don't think so.
C: O.K. And now, this package. What's inside?
W: Just some books and household goods. My daughter's working in Venezuela, and she wanted me to send her some things.
C: O.K. Do you want to send it surface mail or air mail?
W: What's the difference in cost and time?
C: Surface mail would be $12.50 and would take from two to three months. Air mail would be $34.25, but would be there within one to two weeks.

W: Hmmm... well, she said she needed some things right away, so I better send it air mail. Also, there are some fragile things inside, so can you mark it fragile?
C: O.K. Would you like to insure this package?
W: Yes, I think so.
C: O.K. Could you please fill out this insurance form and this Customs' declaration as well.
W: O.K. *(She fills out the forms)* Here.
C: Let's see now. This package is $34.25 plus $2.50 for insurance, plus $1.25 for this other package and 96¢ for the letter. It all comes to $38.96.
W: That's quite a lot, isn't it? Here you are.
C: And $1.04 is your change. Thank you. Have a nice day.
W: Yes You, too.

3 *A secretary wants to send some office mail. She is helped by a post office clerk.*

C: Can I help the next person, please.
S: Yes. I want to send a certified letter.
C: O.K. Do you want a return receipt?
S: Yes, I would.
C: O.K. That will be 85¢, plus $1.00 for the certified mail and 35¢ for the return receipt. That comes to $2.20. Please fill out this return card.
S: *(She fills out the card)* Is this all right?
C: That looks fine.
S: Here you are. And I also want to mail these letters, too.
C: *(Taking the other letters)* I'll take care of these for you. And here's your change.
S: Thank you.
C: Have a nice day.

4 *A man wants to buy a money order. He is served by a clerk.*

C: This window is now open. Can I help someone?
M: Yes. I want to buy a $75.00 money order.
C: Yes, sir. Please fill this out.
M: *(Filling it out)* O.K. Here it is.
C: That will be $75.00 plus 75¢ for the money-order fee .... That comes to $75.75 in total.
M: Here you are.
C: O.K. Thank you. Have a nice day.
M: You too.

C SUGGESTED ACTIVITIES (Discuss and Perform)

If you were in the following situations, what would you do?

1 You want to mail some letters to friends, but you don't have enough stamps at home. You go to buy some.
2 You want to send a package to a friend in another country. You take it to the post office.
3 A man wants to order a set of books through the mail. He doesn't have a checking account, so he needs to send a money order. The books are $22.50.

D – 1 Travel Agency

A EXAMPLES (Read, Discuss and Practice)

There's a PWA *flight leaving
. . . . at . . . . . . and arriving
in . . . . at . . . .*
Halden Airways *has a flight to* Las Vegas.
*That flight departs at . . . . . . and arrives
in . . . . at . . . .*
There is no direct flight to Martinsdale.
You'll have to change planes in Salt Lake City.
*You need to connect to
. . . .*
Would you like first-class or coach?
The fare is $345.67.
Would you like me to make hotel reservations too?
A double room *at the* Highlands *will be* $42.50 a night plus tax.
Would you also need to reserve a rental car?
Do you also need a rental car?

*Can you give me information on a flight to
. . . . ?*
*Is there a direct flight from
. . . . to . . . . ?*
I'd like to make reservations on a flight to . . . .
*What time does it get into
. . . . ?*
Is there a night flight?
What is the fare?
How much is the fare?
Are there any special fares I can get?
Can you make hotel reservations for me?
How much is the hotel a night?
I'd also like to rent a car.
How much would it cost to rent a car?

B MODELS (Read, Discuss and Perform)

1 A young married couple are talking to a travel agent.

- **TA:** Good afternoon. Can I help you?
- **H:** Yes. We're interested in going to San Francisco, and we'd like some information about plane fares and hotels.
- **TA:** O.K. Please have a seat here. When do you want to go?
- **W:** We'd like to leave on Saturday, May 2 and return on Sunday, May 10.
- **TA:** O.K. That would be eight nights and nine days. Is there any particular airline you'd like to fly?
- **H:** No, none in particular.
- **TA:** O.K. There's a PWA flight leaving Houston at 10:45 in the morning that arrives in San Francisco at 12:38.
- **W:** Hmmm . . . that sounds O.K.

TA: And a return flight to Houston would leave San Francisco at 3:45 in the afternoon and arrive here at 6:25.
H: Do you have an earlier one than that?
TA: Of course. How about one leaving San Francisco at 12:20 and arriving here at 2:34?
H: That's better.
TA: O.K. Do you have a place to stay in San Francisco?
W: No. We were hoping you could suggest a place.
TA: Of course. Would you be interested in a luxury hotel or a more moderately priced one?
H: A moderately priced one would be fine.
TA: O.K. A place we've often sent people to is the Brownstone Hotel. A double room would be $35.00 a night plus tax. It's in a very convenient location.
W: That sounds fine, doesn't it dear?
H: Yes. That'll be fine.
TA: Is there anything else you'll need? A rental car, for instance?
W: Yes. We'll need a car for a week. Can you reserve one for us?
TA: Certainly. Bay Area Rent-a-Car has a one week special with unlimited mileage for $175.00 a week. How does that sound?
H: That seems to be O.K.
TA: O.K. I'll start working on these arrangements today, and I'll call you some time tommorrow, if that's convenient.
W: Yes. I'll be home all day. Can you tell us about how much the plane fare, hotel and rental car are going to come to?
TA: Surely. The plane fare will be about $187.00 per person round trip, that's $374.00. The hotel will be . . . let's see . . . $280.00 plus tax . . . about $300.00. The rental car will be another $175.00 or so . . . . That all comes to about . . . $850.00. I can let you know exactly how much it will be when I call tomorrow.
W: That sounds pretty good, doesn't it, Harry?
H: Yeah. That's fine.
TA: O.K. What are your names and your addresses?
W: Robert and Jennifer Shaw. 143 E. Martin Street, Houston.
TA: And your phone number?
W: 253-9264.
TA: O.K. It'll probably be tomorrow afternoon. Thank you for coming to Sunshine Travel.
W: And thank you for your help.

2 *The travel agent calls the couple's home the next day.*

W: Hello. Shaw residence.
TA: Hello, Mrs Shaw. This is Marge from Sunshine Travel calling to say that your San Francisco tickets and reservations are ready.
W: O.K. Can you tell me exactly how much everthing came to?
TA: Yes. It all came to $879.76.
W: O.K. I'll be in to pick everything up tomorrow morning.
TA: That would be fine. Thank you.
W: Thank you.

3 The wife goes to the travel agency to pick up the tickets.

TA: Can I help you?
W: Yes. I'm here to pick up my tickets and reservations for San Francisco. The name is Shaw.
TA: Yes. Here they are. That will be $879.76.
W: O.K. *(Writing out the check)* Here you are.
TA: Thank you. Have a nice trip. And don't hesitate to call on us again if we can be of any help.
W: We will. See you again.
TA: Goodbye now.

C SUGGESTED ACTIVITIES (Discuss and Perform)

How would you handle the following situations?

1 You're studying in America, and you want to take a trip to Mexico City. You go to a travel agency.
2 You get a call from the agency saying your tickets are ready.
3 You go to the agency to pick up your tickets.

D – 2 Check-In / Ticket Counter

A EXAMPLES (Read, Discuss and Practice)

Next please.
Can I help the next person?
What flight are you on?
What's your flight number?
Where are you going?
May I have your ticket.
Ticket, please.
May I see your passport?
Do you want smoking or non-smoking?
Do you want a window or aisle seat?
Is that one-way or round trip?

When is the next bus to Dallas?
What time is your next bus to . . .?
Do you have a flight to Portland?
How much is the fare to Memphis?
What's the fare to Los Angeles?
I'd like a one-way ticket to Houston.
Let me have a round-trip ticket to Fort Lauderdale.
What gate does it leave from?
What's the platform number?
I'd like a seat in the non-smoking section.
I'd like a window seat.
I'd like to make reservations on a train to . . . .

B MODELS (Read, Discuss and Practice)

1 A woman is checking in with the clerk at the airport airline counter.

C: Next, please. What flight are you on?
W: I'm on the flight to Boston. Flight number 72, I think.
C: O.K. May I have your ticket, please?
W: Here you are.
C: Is that smoking or non-smoking you want?
W: Non-smoking. I'd also like a seat near the window.
C: O.K. Here you are. Seat number 47H. Your flight will be boarding at gate E12 at 11:45. Now, where are your bags?
W: Here they are. I'm going to carry this one on with me.
C: O.K. Here are your baggage tickets and boarding pass. Please be at the gate ten minutes before boarding.
W: O.K. Thanks.

2 A young man wants to take a stand-by flight to Chicago. He speaks to a clerk at the airline desk.

YM: Excuse me. Do you think there'll be any stand-by seats available on your flight to Chicago?
C: There may be. The flight is pretty full and people are still checking in. Let me have your name, and I'll call you if there is any space available.
YM: O.K. The name is Murry. John Murry.

(Later)

C: Mr Murry?
YM: Yes.
C: We do have a couple of stand-by seats available to Chicago. Do you still want one?

YM: Yes, I do.
C: O.K. That will be $47.50.
YM: O.K. Here you are.
C: How many bags do you have?
YM: Just this one. This one's a carry-on.
C: O.K. Here's your boarding pass. You're in Seat 84B. Your flight leaves in ten minutes from gate 47. You'd better hurry.
YM: O.K. Thanks.

3 *A man calls a bus station for information. A clerk answers.*

C: Good afternoon. Graybird Bus Company.
M: Hello. Do you have a bus that goes from here in Louisville to Palinstown?
C: Yes. We have two busses a day — one at 10:30 in the morning and one at 3:30 in the afternoon.
M: And how much is the fare?
C: It's $17.68.
M: O.K. Do I need to make reservations?
C: You can If you want, but neither bus is ever very full.
M: O.K. I'll just come by and pick up my ticket when I want to go. Thanks.
C: Thank you for calling Graybird.

4 *A young woman is buying a train ticket from a ticket desk.*

C: Yes, Ma'am. Where to?
YW: I'd like a one-way ticket to Denver.
C: O.K. That'll be $18.80.
YW: Here you are. What platform does the train leave from?
C: It leaves from Platform 12 at 3:43.
YW: Thank you.

C SUGGESTED ACTIVITIES (Discuss and Perform)

How would you handle the following situations?

1 You're going to visit a friend in another city. You're at the airport checking in.
2 You're calling a bus company to find out about busses to another city where a friend of yours lives.
3 You're at the bus station and you want to buy a ticket to a nearby city in order to visit the museum there.

D – 3 Hotels / Motels

A EXAMPLES (Read, Discuss and Practice)

Can I help you?
What kind of room would you like?
When would you like to reserve the room for?
What time will you be arriving?
Do you have a reservation?
Could you please fill out this registration?
The room is $48.50 a night.
The first night is payable in advance.
The bell-hop will take your bags.
Check-out time is 12:00.
What room number is that?
What is your room number?
Your bill comes to $135.50.

I'd like to make reservations for the nights of May 2nd and 3rd.
I'd like a single room.
How much is a double room?
I have reservations for a single room. The name is Lee.
What time is check-out time?
I'd like to make a long-distance call to New York.
I'd like to order dinner.
I'd like to check out now.

B MODELS (Read, Discuss and Perform)

1 A woman is calling a hotel clerk for reservations.

    C: Hello. Marsten Motor Hotel.
    W: Hello. I'd like to make reservations for the nights of March 16th, 17th and 18th.
    C: Yes, of course. What kind of room would you like?
    W: I'd like a double room. How much would that be?
    C: A double room is $42.00 a night.
    W: O.K. I'll take it.
    C: What is the name, please?
    W: The name is Morrow . . . M O R R O W. John and Francine.
    C: And what time will you be arriving?
    W: We're planning to arrive around 7:00 in the evening.
    C: Very well, Mam. We'll have your room ready for you. If you're going to be much later than 7:00, please call ahead and have us hold the room.
    W: O.K. We will. Thank you.
    C: Thank you for calling Marsten Motor Hotel.

2 A man arrives at a motel without reservations. He speaks to a booking clerk.

    C: May I help you, Sir?
    M: Yes. I'd like a room for tonight.
    C: Do you have a reservation?
    M: No, I don't.
    C: I'm sorry, Sir. We're completely booked up. There's a big convention in town this week. Most places are booked.
    M: Oh, no. How am I going to find a room?

COMMUNICATING IN ENGLISH VOLUME 3

    C: I think that some places outside of town might have rooms. You can try checking the yellow pages and calling.
    M: Yeah, O.K. I guess I'll have to try that. Thanks anyway.
    C: I'm sorry, Sir. Good luck.

3 *A married couple are checking into a hotel. A clerk attends to them.*

    C: Can I help you?
    H: Yes. We have reservations for a double room for tonight. The name is Wilson.
    C: Just a minute, Sir. Is that Ken Wilson, Mr. and Mrs.?
    W: Yes, it is.
    C: O.K. Please fill out this registration card.
    W: *(She fills it out)* O.K. Here it is.
    C: O.K. The room is $43.50 a night, the first night payable in advance.
    M: You accept traveler's checks, don't you? *(Writing the check)*
    C: Yes, Sir. We do. *(Taking the check)* The bell-hop will show you to your rooms. *(To the bell-hop)* James, please take Mr. and Mrs. Wilson to their room. Room 747.
    BH: Yes, sir. Please come with me . . . .
    W: O.K. Oh, by the way, what time is check-out time?
    C: Check-out time is 12:00.

4 *A bell-hop brings a guest to the room.*

    BH: Here's your room, Sir. Room 1365. *(He opens the door)*
    G: *(Going inside)* Thank you. It seems to be O.K.
    BH: I hope you find everything to your satisfaction. If there's anything you need, don't hesitate to call the front desk or room service. Hope you have a pleasant stay.
    G: *(Giving a tip)* Thank you.
    BH: Thank you, Sir.

5 *A woman calls room service for dinner.*

    RS: Hello. Room service.
    W: Hello. I'm calling from room 768. I would like to order dinner.
    RS: O.K. What would you like to order?
    W: I'd like the roast beef dinner, with mashed potatoes and green beans.
    RS: Would you care for something to drink with dinner?
    W: Ah . . . yes . . . a large glass of milk.
    RS: Any dessert?
    W: A dish of vanilla ice cream.
    RS: Thank you. We'll bring it up in about thirty minutes.
    W: I'll be waiting.

6 *A man stops at the hotel front desk and speaks to the clerk.*

    C: May I help you, Sir?
    M: Yes. Can you call me a taxi?
    C: Yes, Sir. *(He talks on the telephone)* O.K. Sir. One should be here in about five minutes. It will stop in front.
    M: Thank you.

7 *A married couple are checking out of a hotel. They are attended to by a clerk.*

- **C:** May I help you?
- **H:** Yes. We'd like to check out of our room now. And can you have someone get our bags from our room.
- **C:** Very well, Sir. What room number is that?
- **W:** Room 814.
- **C:** O.K. *(To bell-hop)* Frank. Can you get the bags from 814. *(To the guests)* O.K. Now, your bill comes to $153.75. And, let me see, you had two long-distance calls that come to $8.31. In total, that's $162.76.
- **H:** O.K. Janet, can you take care of this while I get the car?
- **W:** Sure. *(To the clerk)* We'd like to put it on our credit card.
- **C:** Very well. *(He prepares the bill)* Here's your card . . . and please sign here.
- **W:** O.K.
- **BH:** Here are your bags. Where would you like them?
- **W:** Can you take them outside, please.
- **BH:** O.K.
- **C:** I sincerely hope you had a pleasant stay. Please come again.
- **W:** We will, the next time we come to town here.

C SUGGESTED ACTIVITIES (Discuss and Perform)

What would you do in the following situations?

1 You're going to visit friends in another city, but you don't want to stay with them. You make hotel reservations.
2 You're driving along the freeway and want a place to stay for the night. You stop at a decent-looking motel.
3 A man is checking into a hotel.
4 You're staying in a hotel, and want to get a bus to another part of town. You ask at the desk for information.
5 You've been in a certain hotel for two nights, but you don't like it and you want to check out and go to another hotel.

D – 4 Rental Cars

A EXAMPLES (Read, Discuss and Practice)

What kind of car are you interested in?
What size car do you want?
Do you want a large, medium, compact or economy car?
Can you please fill out this application?
May I see your license, please?
May I see the credit card you're using?
Do you want the extra insurance on the car?
Is the tank full?
That will be $46.87.

I'd like to rent a car.
I want to rent a car for a few days.
I'd like an economy-sized car.
I'm returning the car I rented here.

B MODELS (Read, Discuss and Perform)

1 A man is renting a car from a clerk at an airport rental agency.

    C: Yes Sir. Can I help you?
    M: Yes. I'm interested in renting a car for about three days.
    C: O.K. What size car would you like?
    M: What are the rates on a compact car?
    C: Our compact cars run $15.00 a day and 15¢ a mile plus gas.
    M: I see. And how much is an economy car?
    C: Those run $13.00 a day and 13¢ a mile plus gas.
    M: I think I'll take the economy car, then.
    C: O.K., Sir. Please fill out this application.

(The man fills out the application)

    M: Excuse me. Here's the application I just filled out.
    C: O.K. Everything looks fine. May I see your driver's license and the credit card you're using?
    M: Sure. Here.
    C: O.K. Everything looks to be in order. Do you want the extra insurance?
    M: Uhm . . . no.
    C: O.K. Then sign here, please. We'll have your car here in a few minutes. Please wait here.
    M: Sure.

(About ten minutes later)

    C: Excuse me, Sir. Your car is here. The driver here will take you to it.
    M: Thanks.
    D: *(He takes him outside)* Here you go. Here're the keys.
    M: This is it, huh? Thanks.
    D: Safe driving.

2 *A woman wants to return a car she's been renting. She is helped by a clerk.*

    C: Can I help you?
    W: Yes. I'm returning a car I rented last week.
    C: O.K. What's the name please?
    W: Harrison. Roberta Harrison.
    C: It was a Chevette, wasn't it?
    W: That's right.
    C: O.K. Just a minute, and I'll check the mileage and gas. Where is it?
    W: It's the red one out front.

(The clerk goes out and checks the car. She returns)

    C: O.K. You drove 132 miles at 14¢ a mile, that's $18.48. The gas gauge is down about 3 gallons, that's $3.75. Add those things onto your rental fee of $87.65 . . . all that comes to . . . $109.88.
    W: O.K. Here's my credit card.
    C: *(Preparing the bill)* O.K. Here's your card . . . and please sign here. This is your copy. And thank you for renting from Apex Rent-a-Car.

C SUGGESTED ACTIVITIES (Discuss and Perform)

What would you do in these situations?

1 You're at the city airport, and you want to rent a car.
2 You've rented a car for two days and you want to return it.

Appendix 1

Preliminary Activities

1 Circle-Square-Triangle/Line-Ups
2 Mirror Reflection
3 Scene/Story-Building
4 Visualizations
5 Sensations and Feelings

During the first few class meetings and at the beginning of each class, you can prepare students for the types of activities they will be involved with in class. The following exercises will help to do so in two ways: instruction-following and imagination-using. Some of them have the students following and giving the kinds of instructions they will need to understand and use while practicing and performing. Other exercises have the students use their imaginations to think of various ways to see and do things, to recall sensations, feelings and actions, and to create scenes, situations and characters in their imagination.

1 Circle-Square-Triangle/Line-Ups

This is a well-known exercise which begins with the teacher asking the students to stand in a group in the center of the room. The teacher then requests them to stand in a circle, without speaking. Using a variety of non-verbal means, the students have to communicate with one another to form themselves into the requested shape. Some people will probably want to talk, and they should be reminded not to. Next, the teacher can ask everyone to change the circle into a square, again without saying anything. After forming the square, the teacher might request a triangle, then a circle or square again. If there are a lot of people, the teacher might ask them to spell out a word — like CAT or BUS.

Another version of this exercise involves the teacher asking students to stand in a line according to height, again without speaking. They are then requested to line up according to month and date of birth: with January 1 at one end and December 31 at the other end of the line. Again, students must do this without speaking. If you want to, you can ask them to line up by the first letter of their last names, number of years of English study, or other ordered bases.

These exercises require a non-verbal communication system, co-operation, and some people taking leadership responsibilities in order to successfully accomplish them.

2 Mirror Reflection

In this fairly well-known exercise, the teacher asks one student to join him or her and to act like a mirror. This means that the student must reflect like a mirror any actions that the teacher performs. For example, the teacher may do some simple things like bending over and touching toes, squatting, grimacing, slowly rising, stretching, yawning and so on. The student must do the same things at the same time in mirror fashion. The two roles can be switched, with the student performing the actions and the teacher reflecting them. Two students can then be asked to do this together, or the class can be divided into pairs, with one person performing a sequence of actions and the other reflecting it.

This exercise involves physical activity, co-ordinated movement, and people having fun.

3 Scene/Story-Building

In this exercise, the teacher instructs students to act out certain everyday-life activities. You may give instructions, or you or the students may be telling a story while one or more people act out the activity. Scene or story building can involve such activities as: making breakfast, writing and mailing a letter, going to the dentist, helping in an accident, or something similar. The actors follow the instructions or the story line, imagining whatever props or other people are necessary. An example of directions you might give for a simple situation are:

1 Go to the kitchen.
2 Open the refrigerator.
3 Take out a carton of milk.
4 Go to the cupboard and take out a glass.
5 Open the milk carton and pour some milk in the glass.
6 Close the milk carton and put it away.
7 Take a sip of milk.
8 Drink down the whole glass at one time.
9 Burp loudly and smile.
10 Go to the sink and wash out the glass.
11 Put the glass in the dish drainer.
12 Leave the kitchen.

This exercise requires students to follow instructions or a story line and to use their imagination. It is easy for the people acting because they don't really have to say anything, unless they are given something to say by the people giving instructions or telling the story.

4 Visualizations

In this exercise, you create multi-sensory pictures in the mind: combining sights, sounds, tastes, smells, touch. Visualizations vary in complexity and action. An example might be:

> "O.K., everyone. Please close your eyes. Relax and close your eyes. Close them gently and relax. Now I want you to see a picture of a box. You see a small box. The box is wrapped in blue paper. There is a ribbon around the box. It is a red ribbon. There is a white bow on top. You see a small box wrapped in blue paper. It has a red ribbon with a white bow on top The box is on a table. The table is in your home. You are sitting at the

table. You are looking at the box. You want to open the box. You are at home, sitting at the table, looking at the box. You want to open it. You take off the bow. You take off the ribbon. Now you slowly unwrap the paper. You can hear the paper. The paper is making a crinkling sound. Now the paper is off the box. You begin to open the box. You look inside it. You see a children's toy inside. It has a pleasant smell. You take out the toy and begin to play with it. You are playing with it.

Now, I want you to come back to the class-room. You hear my voice. You hear other sounds in the room. You are in the room. Now, open your eyes . . . ."

You can talk about a number of things after the visualization: the size of the box, the room where they were, the toy that was in the box and so on.

In preparing visualizations, it is important to create scenes or story lines that are specific enough to focus on, but general enough to fit within everyone's imagination. The key is to find common cultural or human experiences, and to build around those. It is also a good idea to prepare students for any new or unusual vocabulary ahead of time, because it's very hard to do that within the visualization.

This exercise helps build the ability to imagine the people, situations and settings that will be necessary in later activities when they perform the Examples, Models and Suggested Activities for each lesson.

5 Sensations and Feelings

In this exercise, learners are asked to remember situations where they experienced certain physical sensations or emotions. These can be such things as: feeling cold, feeling hot and sweaty, feeling tired, having a stomache-ache, feeling angry or lonely or happy or afraid and so on. They are asked to recall the situation and, in particular, how the sensation or feeling showed itself in their behavior. People can be helped to recall the sensations or emotions through a series of questions, such as:

Can you remember a time when you felt really . . . . ?
When was it?
Where were you?
Were you alone or with other people?
What were you doing? What were other people doing?
What happened to make you feel that way?
How did you show that you were . . . . ?

The first few times through, it's best to work with physical sensations and pleasant emotions. Once they become familiar with the exercise, students will generally select experiences that reveal as much or as little about themselves as they want to when they talk about them afterwards. Working with emotions such as anger, disappointment, depression, jealousy, etc., can be a little problematic. However, they can also contribute to a very special group feeling if everyone involved has a sensitivity towards and a sincere interest in working with and helping one another.

This exercise works on the more affective elements in practicing and performing the Examples, Models and Suggested Activities. The activities in Appendix 2 can be used for practicing and performing the Examples, Models and Suggested Activities. An important point is that people should not be asked to act out physical sensations and emotions. Rather, they should be asked to remember how they felt when they experienced a particular sensation or emotion, and they should try to put that feeling into what they're saying and doing. In so doing, the practicing and performing will be more "genuine", and the genuineness will help people learn what it is important to learn in the Practice and Perform parts.

Appendix 2

Suggested Techniques

1. Interpretative Reading
2. Talk and Listen
3. Skits/Improvised Role-Playing
4. Conversations on Blackboard
5. Questions on Papers
6. Values Clarification
7. Taped Natural Conversations/Movies

The seven techniques explained in Appendix 2 can be used in the Practice and Perform stages of the Examples, Models and Suggested Activities. You can use them to help students actively learn the things they've read, thought about and discussed in previous stages. Since all of these techniques involve students actively working with other students, it is a good idea to prepare students for these techniques by using the preliminary activities explained in Appendix 1.

1 Interpretative Reading

Simply stated, the interpretative reading is reading a line, script or story in the same way that a particular person in a particular situation would say it. You read it with the same intonation, stress, emotional quality and speed as that person would use. There is no physical movement with interpretative reading. The reader sits or stands in one place. Everthing is conveyed through the reader's voice and the intonation, stress, emotional quality and speed that reader uses.

Interpretative reading can be used to practice or perform the Examples, Models and Suggested Activities. In the Examples section, after students understand the meaning and context of the examples, you can ask them to interpretatively read the examples. Similarly, after the models have been read and discussed, you can ask one or more students to interpretatively read the models. Lastly, if you have asked students to write skits in the Suggested Activities section, you can ask them to read these interpretatively before they actually perform them.

Success in using this technique depends on students understanding the meaning and context of things said in the Examples and Models. If they don't understand the meaning of certain words or expressions, or if they don't understand the time, place, people, people's intentions and feelings, it will be very difficult to do interpretative reading. If these things have become clear in the Read and Discuss stages, students will have much less difficulty. In addition, the more they use and get used to the technique, the better they become at it.

2 Talk and Listen

Richard Via, in his book *English in Three Acts**,* discusses "talk and listen" as a technique actors sometimes use to learn parts in a play. The procedure involves the following things:

(a) dividing a dialogue or script into parts and writing the different parts on separate cards or pieces of paper,
(b) performers looking at and listening to the other person while the other person is speaking,
(c) the performer's establishing eye-contact with the other person when the performer is speaking to the other person.

Of course, it is important that the performers understand the time, place, people, people's intentions and feelings, of the situation. These things should become clear during the "Read and Discuss" stages of working with the lessons.

Talk and listen cards might look as follows:

Dialogue
A branch manager is meeting a Vice-President at the airport.

BM: Good afternoon, Mr Browning. Welcome to Martinstown.
VP: Thank you, Les.
BM: How was your flight?
VP: Oh, not bad. It was a little rough in places, but . . .

Talk and Listen Card   1
A branch manager is meeting a Vice-President at the airport.

BM: Good afternoon, Mr Browning. Welcome to Martinstown.
VP:
BM: How was your flight?
VP:

Talk and Listen Card   2
A branch manager is meeting a Vice-President at the airport.

BM:
VP: Thank you, Les.
BM:
VP: Oh, not bad. It was a little rough in places, but . . .

The reason for putting the two parts on two separate cards is to provide students with some help but, at the same time, to prevent them from just reading the lines without listening to the other person. When students are performing, they should not be reading the cards: they should be looking at and listening to each other. The cards serve as memory jogs, so that memorizing the dialogues is not necessary. The substitution of alternative

---

*Via, Richard A. *English in Three Acts* The University of Hawaii Press, 1976. See also: Via, Richard A. and Larry Smith, *Talk and Listen* Pergamon Press, 1983.

ways to say the same thing is fine, as long as they are appropriate to the situation. Students can also be encouraged to continue the situation beyond what is on the card.

Via points out that if people are not listening to each other, you can get them to listen closely by changing a part to make it incongruous. For example, if the person playing the businessman's part above is not listening, you can change the VP's part like this:

Talk and Listen Card   2
A stranger comes up to you and begins talking.

BM:
VP: My name isn't Browning. And who are you?
BM:
VP: I told you my name isn't Browning. You're making a mistake.

3 Skits/Improvised Role-Playing

Skits and Improvised Role-Playing can be used with the "Suggested Activities" section of each lesson. In doing Skits, students discuss and write out scripts for the situation. They then use the scripts in performing. In doing improvised role-playing, students discuss the situation and then perform it without writing scripts. Skits can be useful first steps to improvised role-playing, or can be used if the situation is rather long and complicated. Improvised role-playing more closely approximates the ability to use what they're learning in everyday life outside of class, and, thus, are a more valuable type of exercise.

As with "interpretative reading" and "talk and listen", students need a good understanding of the context of the situation: the time, place, people and people's intentions and feelings. If students have a clear image of the situation and people and people's behavior, they'll be able to perform more naturally and creatively. For this reason, working on the preliminary activities given in Appendix 1 will be a great help to students when they reach the practice and performing stages in the Examples, Models and Suggested Activities.

4 Conversations on Blackboard

A fairly simple but effective conversation exercise is to have a conversation with a student on the blackboard. You can begin by asking a student to come and join you at the board. Give him/her a piece of chalk, and without saying another word, write the opening question or statement of the conversation on the board. Have the student understand they need to respond to it. Make it clear that he/she doesn't have to do so completely by him/herself. Encourage other students who are watching the conversation to help or correct the student at the board when needed. After finishing the conversation, practice reading it with him/her. You can also erase some of the lines and explore other ways of saying things or having the conversation grow.

This is a particularly good exercise for concentrating on the mechanisms of conversations. It is also good for showing how the conversations techniques presented in Chapter 1 can be used. Because the conversation is on the chalkboard, students can see how things relate to and are built upon one another as the conversation grows. As they get used to the technique, students can also start having conversations with each other in this way.

5 Questions on Papers

This is another simple exercise which can be used for getting conversations started in class. Have students sit in groups of four or five people. Give each person a small piece of paper or an index card. Ask them to write a question on the piece of paper. Tell them that any question is O.K., as long as it's a question they wouldn't mind being asked and having to answer themselves. You might also point out that open-ended questions lead to more to talk about than yes-no questions.

After they write the questions, tell them to fold the papers and put them in the center of the table or in a box. People then take turns drawing a paper with a question and answering it. Other students should be trying to help the person answer it and build a conversation, using some of the conversation techiques in Chapter 1. After everyone has had a turn, then they are finished or they can go on to another round. One variation of the exercise is to use statements on the papers instead of questions.

6 Values Clarification

Values clarification exercises are another very effective way of stimulating conversation and discussion in class. They are effective, if used properly, because they get people talking about issues and concerns that are important to them personally. There are a number of different types of exercises that can be used, some examples of which are given in Lesson 2 of Chapter 1. Numerous books and journal articles have been written explaining this technique and giving examples of different exercises that can be used.

The important thing to keep in mind is the need for a balance between pure conversation and conversation where students also bring some of the things they're learning into the conversations. It's a difficult balance to strike: making it useful without making it artificial. Stopping a conversation to make a point can kill it after that. As alternatives, it is possible to take notes on particular things and talk about them afterwards, or else to tape-record the conversations, if students feel comfortable with such a procedure.

7 Taped Natural Conversations/Movies

One other useful technique involves bringing in tape-recorded samples of natural conversations. From listening to these samples, students can gain other insights into conversation dynamics. If the conversations are at natural speed, students may find it quite difficult to understand some things. But listening to it again on replay, or having students try to guess what was probably said, based on what they did understand can be very helpful. Movies can also be used if you have the equipment to work them in class. They may take a longer time, but since they have a story-line behind them, students find it easier and easier to understand as they understand the story and get used to the actors. The biggest challenge is to find a movie that is natural, easy and interesting enough to capture student's attention and energy.

NOTES

NOTES

NOTES

NOTES

NOTES

Printed in Great Britain by A. Wheaton & Co. Ltd., Exeter